# PHRASEBOOK

## — POLISH —

By Andrey Taranov

# THE MOST IMPORTANT PHRASES

This phrasebook contains
the most important
phrases and questions
for basic communication
Everything you need
to survive overseas

Phrasebook + 250-word dictionary

# English-Polish phrasebook & mini dictionary

By Andrey Taranov

The collection of "Everything Will Be Okay" travel phrasebooks published by T&P Books is designed for people traveling abroad for tourism and business. The phrasebooks contain what matters most - the essentials for basic communication. This is an indispensable set of phrases to "survive" while abroad.

You'll also find a mini dictionary with 250 useful words required for everyday communication - the names of months and days of the week, measurements, family members, and more.

T&P Books Publishing
www.tpbooks.com

ISBN: 978-1-78492-416-4

This book is also available in E-book formats.
Please visit www.tpbooks.com or the major online bookstores.

# FOREWORD

The collection of "Everything Will Be Okay" travel phrasebooks published by T&P Books is designed for people traveling abroad for tourism and business. The phrasebooks contain what matters most - the essentials for basic communication. This is an indispensable set of phrases to "survive" while abroad.

This phrasebook will help you in most cases where you need to ask something, get directions, find out how much something costs, etc. It can also resolve difficult communication situations where gestures just won't help.

This book contains a lot of phrases that have been grouped according to the most relevant topics. You'll also find a mini dictionary with useful words - numbers, time, calendar, colors...

Take "Everything Will Be Okay" phrasebook with you on the road and you'll have an irreplaceable traveling companion who will help you find your way out of any situation and teach you to not fear speaking with foreigners.

# TABLE OF CONTENTS

T&P Books Publishing

# PRONUNCIATION

| Letter | Polish example | T&P phonetic alphabet | English example |
|--------|----------------|-----------------------|-----------------|

## Vowels

| Letter | Polish example | T&P phonetic alphabet | English example |
|--------|----------------|-----------------------|-----------------|
| A a | fala | [a] | shorter than in ask |
| Ą ą | są | [ɔ̃] | strong |
| E e | tekst | [ɛ] | man, bad |
| Ę ę | pięć | [ɛ] | fang |
| I i | niski | [i] | shorter than in feet |
| O o | strona | [ɔ] | bottle, doctor |
| Ó ó | ołów | [u] | book |
| U u | ulica | [u] | book |
| Y y | stalowy | [ɪ] | big, America |

## Consonants

| Letter | Polish example | T&P phonetic alphabet | English example |
|--------|----------------|-----------------------|-----------------|
| B b | brew | [b] | baby, book |
| C c | palec | [ts] | cats, tsetse fly |
| Ć ć | haftować | [tʃ] | church, French |
| D d | modny | [d] | day, doctor |
| F f | perfumy | [f] | face, food |
| G g | zegarek | [g] | game, gold |
| H h | handel | [h] | huge, hat |
| J j | jajko | [j] | yes, New York |
| K k | krab | [k] | clock, kiss |
| L l | mleko | [l] | lace, people |
| Ł ł | głodny | [w] | vase, winter |
| M m | guma | [m] | magic, milk |
| N n | Indie | [n] | name, normal |
| Ń ń | jesień | [ɲ] | canyon, new |
| P p | poczta | [p] | pencil, private |
| R r | portret | [r] | rice, radio |
| S s | studnia | [s] | city, boss |
| Ś ś | świat | [ɕ] | sheep, shop |

| Letter | Polish example | T&P phonetic alphabet | English example |
|--------|----------------|----------------------|-----------------|
| T t | taniec | [t] | tune, student |
| W w | wieczór | [v] | very, river |
| Z z | zachód | [z] | zebra, please |
| Ź ź | żaba | [z̊] | gigolo |
| Ż ż | żagiel | [ʒ] | forge, pleasure |

## Combinations of letters

| ch | ich, zachód | [h] | huge, humor |
|----|-------------|-----|-------------|
| ci | kwiecień | [tʃ] | cheese |
| cz | czasami | [tʃ] | church, French |
| dz | dzbanek | [dz] | beads, kids |
| dzi | dziecko | [dz̊] | jeans, gene |
| dź | dźwig | [dz̊] | jeans, gene |
| dż | dżinsy | [j] | yes, New York |
| ni | niedziela | [ɲ] | canyon, new |
| rz | orzech | [ʒ] | forge, pleasure |
| si | osiem | [ɕ] | sheep, shop |
| sz | paszport | [ʃ] | machine, shark |
| zi | zima | [z̊] | gigolo |

## Comments

Letters Qq, Vv, Xx used in foreign loanwords only

# LIST OF ABBREVIATIONS

## English abbreviations

| | | |
|---|---|---|
| ab. | - | about |
| adj | - | adjective |
| adv | - | adverb |
| anim. | - | animate |
| as adj | - | attributive noun used as adjective |
| e.g. | - | for example |
| etc. | - | et cetera |
| fam. | - | familiar |
| fem. | - | feminine |
| form. | - | formal |
| inanim. | - | inanimate |
| masc. | - | masculine |
| math | - | mathematics |
| mil. | - | military |
| n | - | noun |
| pl | - | plural |
| pron. | - | pronoun |
| sb | - | somebody |
| sing. | - | singular |
| sth | - | something |
| v aux | - | auxiliary verb |
| vi | - | intransitive verb |
| vi, vt | - | intransitive, transitive verb |
| vt | - | transitive verb |

## Polish abbreviations

| | | |
|---|---|---|
| ż | - | feminine noun |
| ż, l.mn. | - | feminine plural |
| l.mn. | - | plural |
| m | - | masculine noun |
| m, ż | - | masculine, feminine |
| m, l.mn. | - | masculine plural |
| n | - | neuter |

# POLISH PHRASEBOOK

This section contains
important phrases that may
come in handy in various
real-life situations.
The phrasebook will help
you ask for directions, clarify
a price, buy tickets, and
order food at a restaurant

**T&P Books Publishing**

# PHRASEBOOK CONTENTS

T&P Books Publishing

# The bare minimum

Excuse me, …

**Przepraszam, …**
[pʃɛ'praʃam, …]

Hello.

**Witam.**
['vʲitam]

Thank you.

**Dziękuję.**
[dʑiɛɲ'kujɛ]

Good bye.

**Do widzenia.**
[dɔ vʲi'dzɛɲa]

Yes.

**Tak.**
[tak]

No.

**Nie.**
[ɲɛ]

I don't know.

**Nie wiem.**
[ɲɛ 'vʲɛm]

Where? | Where to? | When?

**Gdzie? | Dokąd? | Kiedy?**
[gdʑɛ? | 'dɔkɔnt? | 'kʲɛdi?]

I need …

**Potrzebuję …**
[pɔtʃɛ'bujɛ …]

I want …

**Chcę …**
['xtsɛ …]

Do you have …?

**Czy jest …?**
[tʃi 'jɛst …?]

Is there a … here?

**Czy jest tutaj …?**
[tʃi 'jɛst 'tutaj …?]

May I …?

**Czy mogę …?**
[tʃi 'mɔgɛ …?]

…, please (polite request)

**…, poproszę**
[…, pɔ'prɔʃɛ]

I'm looking for …

**Szukam …**
['ʃukam …]

restroom

**toalety**
[tɔa'lɛti]

ATM

**bankomatu**
[bankɔ'matu]

pharmacy (drugstore)

**apteki**
[a'ptɛkʲi]

hospital

**szpitala**
[ʃpʲi'tala]

police station

**komendy policji**
[kɔ'mɛndi pɔ'ʎitsji]

subway

**metra**
['mɛtra]

| | |
|---|---|
| taxi | **taksówki**<br>[ta'ksufkʲi] |
| train station | **dworca kolejowego**<br>['dvɔrtsa kɔlɛjɔ'vɛgɔ] |
| My name is … | **Mam na imię …**<br>[mam na 'imʲiɛ …] |
| What's your name? | **Jak pan /pani/ ma na imię?**<br>['jak pan /'paɲi/ ma na 'imʲiɛ?] |
| Could you please help me? | **Czy może pan /pani/ mi pomóc?**<br>[tʃi 'mɔʒɛ pan /'paɲi/ mʲi 'pɔmuts?] |
| I've got a problem. | **Mam problem.**<br>[mam 'prɔblɛm] |
| I don't feel well. | **Źle się czuję.**<br>[zlɛ ɕɛ 'tʃujɛ] |
| Call an ambulance! | **Proszę wezwać karetkę!**<br>['prɔʃɛ 'vɛzvatɕ ka'rɛtkɛ!] |
| May I make a call? | **Czy mogę zadzwonić?**<br>[tʃi 'mɔgɛ za'dzvɔɲitɕ?] |
| I'm sorry. | **Przepraszam.**<br>[pʃɛ'praʃam] |
| You're welcome. | **Proszę bardzo.**<br>['prɔʃɛ 'bardzɔ] |

| | |
|---|---|
| I, me | **ja**<br>['ja] |
| you (inform.) | **ty**<br>['ti] |
| he | **on**<br>[ɔn] |
| she | **ona**<br>['ɔna] |
| they (masc.) | **oni**<br>['ɔɲi] |
| they (fem.) | **one**<br>['ɔnɛ] |
| we | **my**<br>['mi] |
| you (pl) | **wy**<br>['vi] |
| you (sg, form.) | **pan /pani/**<br>[pan /'paɲi/] |

| | |
|---|---|
| ENTRANCE | **WEJŚCIE**<br>['vɛjɕtɕɛ] |
| EXIT | **WYJŚCIE**<br>['vijɕtɕɛ] |
| OUT OF ORDER | **NIECZYNNY**<br>[ɲɛ'tʃinni] |
| CLOSED | **ZAMKNIĘTE**<br>[za'mkɲiɛntɛ] |

OPEN

**OTWARTE**
[ɔˈtfartɛ]

FOR WOMEN

**PANIE**
[ˈpaɲɛ]

FOR MEN

**PANOWIE**
[paˈnɔvʲɛ]

# Questions

| | |
|---|---|
| Where? | **Gdzie?**<br>['gdʑɛ?] |
| Where to? | **Dokąd?**<br>['dɔkɔnt?] |
| Where from? | **Skąd?**<br>['skɔnt?] |
| Why? | **Dlaczego?**<br>[dla'tʃɛgɔ?] |
| For what reason? | **Dlaczego?**<br>[dla'tʃɛgɔ?] |
| When? | **Kiedy?**<br>['kʲɛdi?] |

| | |
|---|---|
| How long? | **Jak długo?**<br>['jag 'dwugɔ?] |
| At what time? | **O której godzinie?**<br>[ɔ 'kturɛj gɔ'dʑiɲɛ?] |
| How much? | **Ile kosztuje?**<br>['ilɛ kɔ'ʃtujɛ?] |
| Do you have ...? | **Czy jest ...?**<br>[tʃi 'jɛst ...?] |
| Where is ...? | **Gdzie jest ...?**<br>[gdʑɛ 'jɛst ...?] |

| | |
|---|---|
| What time is it? | **Która godzina?**<br>['ktura gɔ'dʑina?] |
| May I make a call? | **Czy mogę zadzwonić?**<br>[tʃi 'mɔgɛ za'dzvɔɲitɕ?] |
| Who's there? | **Kto tam?**<br>[ktɔ tam?] |
| Can I smoke here? | **Czy mogę tu zapalić?**<br>[tʃi 'mɔgɛ tu za'paʎitɕ?] |
| May I ...? | **Czy mogę ...?**<br>[tʃi 'mɔgɛ ...?] |

# Needs

| | |
|---|---|
| I'd like ... | **Chciałbym /Chciałabym/** ...<br>['xtɕawbim /xtɕa'wabim/ ...] |
| I don't want ... | **Nie chcę ...**<br>[ɲɛ 'xtsɛ ...] |
| I'm thirsty. | **Jestem spragniony /spragniona/.**<br>['jɛstɛm spra'gɲɔni /spra'gɲɔna/] |
| I want to sleep. | **Chce mi się spać.**<br>['xtsɛ mʲi ɕiɛ 'spatɕ] |

| | |
|---|---|
| I want ... | **Chcę ...**<br>['xtsɛ ...] |
| to wash up | **umyć się**<br>['umitɕ ɕiɛ] |
| to brush my teeth | **umyć zęby**<br>['umitɕ 'zɛmbi] |
| to rest a while | **trochę odpocząć**<br>['trɔxɛ ɔ'tpɔtʃɔntɕ] |
| to change my clothes | **zmienić ubranie**<br>['zmʲɛɲitɕ u'braɲɛ] |

| | |
|---|---|
| to go back to the hotel | **wrócić do hotelu**<br>['vrutɕitɕ dɔ xɔ'tɛlu] |
| to buy ... | **kupić ...**<br>['kupʲitɕ ...] |
| to go to ... | **iść ...**<br>['iɕtɕ ...] |
| to visit ... | **odwiedzić ...**<br>[ɔ'dvʲɛdʑitɕ ...] |
| to meet with ... | **spotkać się z ...**<br>['spɔtkatɕ ɕiɛ s ...] |
| to make a call | **zadzwonić**<br>[za'dzvɔɲitɕ] |

| | |
|---|---|
| I'm tired. | **Jestem zmęczony /zmęczona/.**<br>['jɛstɛm zmɛ'ntʃɔni /zmɛ'ntʃɔna/] |
| We are tired. | **Jesteśmy zmęczeni /zmęczone/.**<br>[jɛs'tɛɕmi zmɛ'ntʃɛɲi /zmɛ'ntʃɔnɛ/] |
| I'm cold. | **Jest mi zimno.**<br>['jɛst mʲi 'ʑimnɔ] |
| I'm hot. | **Jest mi gorąco.**<br>['jɛst mʲi gɔ'rɔntsɔ] |
| I'm OK. | **W porządku.**<br>[f pɔ'ʒɔntku] |

I need to make a call.

**Muszę zadzwonić.**
['muʃɛ za'dzvɔɲitɕ]

I need to go to the restroom.

**Muszę iść do toalety.**
['muʃɛ 'iɕtɕ dɔ tɔa'lɛti]

I have to go.

**Muszę iść.**
['muʃɛ 'iɕtɕ]

I have to go now.

**Muszę już iść.**
['muʃɛ 'juʒ 'iɕtɕ]

## Asking for directions

| | |
|---|---|
| Excuse me, ... | **Przepraszam, ...**<br>[pʃɛ'praʃam, ...] |
| Where is ...? | **Gdzie jest ...?**<br>[gdʑɛ 'jɛst ...?] |
| Which way is ...? | **W którą stronę jest ...?**<br>[f 'kturɔ̃ 'strɔnɛ 'jɛst ...?] |
| Could you help me, please? | **Czy może pan /pani/ mi pomóc?**<br>[tʃi 'mɔʒɛ pan /'paɲi/ mʲi 'pɔmuts?] |
| I'm looking for ... | **Szukam ...**<br>['ʃukam ...] |
| I'm looking for the exit. | **Szukam wyjścia.**<br>['ʃukam 'vɨjɕtɕa] |
| I'm going to ... | **Jadę do ...**<br>['jadɛ dɔ ...] |
| Am I going the right way to ...? | **Czy idę w dobrym kierunku do ...?**<br>[tʃi 'idɛ v 'dɔbrɨm kʲɛ'runku 'dɔ ...?] |
| Is it far? | **Czy to daleko?**<br>[tʃi tɔ da'lɛkɔ?] |
| Can I get there on foot? | **Czy mogę tam dojść pieszo?**<br>[tʃi 'mɔgɛ tam 'dɔjɕtɕ 'pʲɛʃɔ?] |
| Can you show me on the map? | **Czy może mi pan /pani/ pokazać na mapie?**<br>[tʃi 'mɔʒɛ mʲi pan /'paɲi/ pɔ'kazatɕ na 'mapʲɛ?] |
| Show me where we are right now. | **Proszę mi pokazać gdzie teraz jesteśmy.**<br>['prɔʃɛ mʲi pɔ'kazatɕ gdʑɛ 'tɛras jɛ'stɛɕmi] |
| Here | **Tutaj**<br>['tutaj] |
| There | **Tam**<br>[tam] |
| This way | **Tędy**<br>['tɛndi] |
| Turn right. | **Należy skręcić w prawo.**<br>[na'lɛʒi 'skrɛntɕitɕ f 'pravɔ] |
| Turn left. | **Należy skręcić w lewo.**<br>[na'lɛʒi 'skrɛntɕitɕ v 'lɛvɔ] |
| first (second, third) turn | **pierwszy (drugi, trzeci) skręt**<br>['pʲɛrfʃi ('drugi, 'tʃɛtɕi) 'skrɛnt] |

to the right

**w prawo**
[f 'pravɔ]

to the left

**w lewo**
[v 'lɛvɔ]

Go straight.

**Proszę iść prosto.**
['prɔʃɛ 'iɕtɕ 'prɔstɔ]

# Signs

| | |
|---|---|
| WELCOME! | **WITAMY!** [vʲi'tamɨ] |
| ENTRANCE | **WEJŚCIE** ['vɛjɕtɕɛ] |
| EXIT | **WYJŚCIE** ['vɨjɕtɕɛ] |

| | |
|---|---|
| PUSH | **PCHAĆ** ['pxatɕ] |
| PULL | **CIĄGNĄĆ** ['tɕiɔŋgnɔntɕ] |
| OPEN | **OTWARTE** [ɔ'tfartɛ] |
| CLOSED | **ZAMKNIĘTE** [za'mkɲiɛntɛ] |

| | |
|---|---|
| FOR WOMEN | **PANIE** ['paɲɛ] |
| FOR MEN | **PANOWIE** [pa'nɔvʲɛ] |
| MEN, GENTS | **TOALETA MĘSKA** [tɔa'lɛta 'mɛ̃ska] |
| WOMEN, LADIES | **TOALETA DAMSKA** [tɔa'lɛta 'damska] |

| | |
|---|---|
| DISCOUNTS | **ZNIŻKI** ['zɲiʃkʲi] |
| SALE | **WYPRZEDAŻ** [vʲi'pʃɛdaʒ] |
| FREE | **ZA DARMO** [za 'darmɔ] |
| NEW! | **NOWOŚĆ!** ['nɔvɔɕtɕ!] |
| ATTENTION! | **UWAGA!** [u'vaga!] |

| | |
|---|---|
| NO VACANCIES | **BRAK WOLNYCH MIEJSC** ['brag 'vɔlnix 'mʲɛjsts] |
| RESERVED | **REZERWACJA** [rɛzɛ'rvatsja] |
| ADMINISTRATION | **ADMINISTRACJA** [admʲiɲi'stratsja] |
| STAFF ONLY | **TYLKO DLA PERSONELU** ['tilkɔ 'dla pɛrsɔ'nɛlu] |

| | |
|---|---|
| BEWARE OF THE DOG! | **UWAGA PIES**<br>[u'vaga 'pɨɛs] |
| NO SMOKING! | **ZAKAZ PALENIA**<br>['zakas pa'lɛɲa] |
| DO NOT TOUCH! | **NIE DOTYKAĆ!**<br>[ɲɛ dɔ'tikatɕ!] |
| DANGEROUS | **NIEBEZPIECZNE**<br>[ɲɛbɛ'spʲɛt͡ʃnɛ] |
| DANGER | **NIEBEZPIECZEŃSTWO**<br>[ɲɛbɛspʲɛ't͡ʃɛɲstfɔ] |
| HIGH VOLTAGE | **WYSOKIE NAPIĘCIE**<br>[vɨ'sɔkʲɛ na'pʲiɛntɕɛ] |
| NO SWIMMING! | **ZAKAZ PŁYWANIA**<br>['zakas pwi'vaɲa] |
| OUT OF ORDER | **NIECZYNNY**<br>[ɲɛ't͡ʃinni] |
| FLAMMABLE | **ŁATWOPALNY**<br>[watfɔ'palni] |
| FORBIDDEN | **ZABRONIONE**<br>[zabrɔ'ɲɔnɛ] |
| NO TRESPASSING! | **WSTĘP WZBRONIONY!**<br>['fstɛmb vzbrɔ'ɲɔni!] |
| WET PAINT | **ŚWIEŻO MALOWANE**<br>['ɕvʲɛʒɔ malɔ'vanɛ] |
| CLOSED FOR RENOVATIONS | **ZAMKNIĘTE NA CZAS REMONTU**<br>[za'mkɲiɛntɛ na 't͡ʃaz rɛ'mɔntu] |
| WORKS AHEAD | **ROBOTY DROGOWE**<br>[rɔ'bɔti drɔ'gɔvɛ] |
| DETOUR | **OBJAZD**<br>['ɔbjazt] |

# Transportation. General phrases

| | |
|---|---|
| plane | **samolot**<br>[sa'mɔlɔt] |
| train | **pociąg**<br>['pɔtɕiɔŋk] |
| bus | **autobus**<br>[aw'tɔbus] |
| ferry | **prom**<br>['prɔm] |
| taxi | **taksówka**<br>[ta'ksufka] |
| car | **samochód**<br>[sa'mɔxut] |

| | |
|---|---|
| schedule | **rozkład jazdy \| rozkład lotów**<br>['rɔskwat 'jazdi \| 'rɔskwat 'lɔtuf] |
| Where can I see the schedule? | **Gdzie znajdę rozkład jazdy?**<br>[gdʑɛ 'znajdɛ 'rɔskwat 'jazdi?] |
| workdays (weekdays) | **dni robocze**<br>['dɲi rɔ'bɔtʃɛ] |
| weekends | **weekend**<br>[vɛ'ɛkɛnt] |
| holidays | **święta**<br>['ɕvʲiɛnta] |

| | |
|---|---|
| DEPARTURE | **WYJAZDY \| PRZYLOTY**<br>[vi'jazdi \| pʃi'lɔti] |
| ARRIVAL | **PRZYJAZDY \| ODLOTY**<br>[pʃi'jazdi \| ɔ'dlɔti] |
| DELAYED | **OPÓŹNIONY**<br>[ɔpu'ʑɲɔni] |
| CANCELED | **ODWOŁANY**<br>[ɔdvɔ'wani] |

| | |
|---|---|
| next (train, etc.) | **następny**<br>[na'stɛmpni] |
| first | **pierwszy**<br>['pʲɛrfʃi] |
| last | **ostatni**<br>[ɔ'statɲi] |

| | |
|---|---|
| When is the next ...? | **O której jest następny ...?**<br>[ɔ 'kturɛj 'jɛst na'stɛmpni ...?] |
| When is the first ...? | **O której jest pierwszy ...?**<br>[ɔ 'kturɛj 'jɛst 'pʲɛrfʃi ...?] |

When is the last ...?

**O której jest ostatni ...?**
[ɔ 'kturɛj 'jɛst ɔ'statɲi ...?]

transfer (change of trains, etc.)

**przesiadka**
[pʃɛ'ɕatka]

to make a transfer

**przesiąść się**
['pʃɛɕiɔ̃ɕtɕ ɕiɛ]

Do I need to make a transfer?

**Czy muszę się przesiadać?**
[tʃɨ 'muʃɛ ɕiɛ pʃɛ'ɕadatɕ?]

# Buying tickets

| | |
|---|---|
| Where can I buy tickets? | **Gdzie mogę kupić bilety?**<br>[gdʑɛ 'mɔgɛ 'kupʲitɕ bʲi'lɛti?] |
| ticket | **bilet**<br>['bʲilɛt] |
| to buy a ticket | **kupić bilet**<br>['kupʲitɕ 'bʲilɛt] |
| ticket price | **cena biletu**<br>['tsɛna bʲi'lɛtu] |

| | |
|---|---|
| Where to? | **Dokąd?**<br>['dɔkɔnt?] |
| To what station? | **Do której stacji?**<br>[dɔ 'kturɛj 'statsji?] |
| I need ... | **Poproszę ...**<br>[pɔ'prɔʃɛ ...] |
| one ticket | **jeden bilet**<br>['jɛdɛn 'bʲilɛt] |
| two tickets | **dwa bilety**<br>['dva bʲi'lɛti] |
| three tickets | **trzy bilety**<br>[t͡ʃi bʲi'lɛti] |

| | |
|---|---|
| one-way | **w jedną stronę**<br>[f 'jɛdnɔ̃ 'strɔnɛ] |
| round-trip | **w obie strony**<br>[v 'ɔbʲɛ 'strɔni] |
| first class | **pierwsza klasa**<br>['pʲɛrfʃa 'klasa] |
| second class | **druga klasa**<br>['druga 'klasa] |

| | |
|---|---|
| today | **dzisiaj**<br>['dʑiɕaj] |
| tomorrow | **jutro**<br>['jutrɔ] |
| the day after tomorrow | **pojutrze**<br>[pɔ'jut͡ʃɛ] |
| in the morning | **rano**<br>['ranɔ] |
| in the afternoon | **po południu**<br>[pɔ pɔ'wudɲu] |
| in the evening | **wieczorem**<br>[vʲɛ't͡ʃɔrɛm] |

| | |
|---|---|
| aisle seat | **miejsce przy przejściu**<br>['mʲɛjstsɛ pʃi 'pʃɛjɕtɕu] |
| window seat | **miejsce przy oknie**<br>['mʲɛjstsɛ pʃi 'ɔkɲɛ] |
| How much? | **Ile kosztuje?**<br>['ilɛ kɔ'ʃtujɛ?] |
| Can I pay by credit card? | **Czy mogę zapłacić kartą?**<br>[tʃi 'mɔgɛ za'pwatɕitɕ 'kartɔ̃?] |

# Bus

| | |
|---|---|
| bus | **autobus**<br>[aw'tɔbus] |
| intercity bus | **autobus międzymiastowy**<br>[aw'tɔbus mʲiɛndzimʲa'stɔvɨ] |
| bus stop | **przystanek autobusowy**<br>[pʃi'stanɛk awtɔbu'sɔvɨ] |
| Where's the nearest bus stop? | **Gdzie jest najbliższy przystanek autobusowy?**<br>[gdʑɛ 'jɛst najb'ʎiʃʃi pʃi'stanɛk awtɔbu'sɔvi?] |

| | |
|---|---|
| number (bus ~, etc.) | **numer**<br>['numɛr] |
| Which bus do I take to get to ...? | **Którym autobusem dojadę do ...?**<br>['kturim awtɔ'busɛm dɔ'jadɛ dɔ ...?] |
| Does this bus go to ...? | **Czy ten autobus jedzie do ...?**<br>[tʃi 'tɛn aw'tɔbus 'jɛdʑɛ dɔ ...?] |
| How frequent are the buses? | **Jak często jeżdżą autobusy?**<br>['jak 'tʃɛ̃stɔ 'jɛʒdʒɔ̃ awtɔ'busɨ?] |

| | |
|---|---|
| every 15 minutes | **co piętnaście minut**<br>['tsɔ pʲiɛ'ntnaɕtɕɛ 'mʲinut] |
| every half hour | **co pół godziny**<br>['tsɔ 'puw gɔ'dʑini] |
| every hour | **co godzinę**<br>['tsɔ gɔ'dʑinɛ] |
| several times a day | **kilka razy dziennie**<br>['kʲilka 'razi 'dʑɛnɲɛ] |
| ... times a day | **... razy dziennie**<br>[... 'razi 'dʑɛnɲɛ] |

| | |
|---|---|
| schedule | **rozkład jazdy**<br>['rɔskwat 'jazdi] |
| Where can I see the schedule? | **Gdzie znajdę rozkład jazdy?**<br>[gdʑɛ 'znajdɛ 'rɔskwat 'jazdi?] |

| | |
|---|---|
| When is the next bus? | **O której jest następny autobus?**<br>[ɔ 'kturɛj 'jɛst na'stɛmpni aw'tɔbus?] |
| When is the first bus? | **O której jest pierwszy autobus?**<br>[ɔ 'kturɛj 'jɛst 'pʲɛrfʃi aw'tɔbus?] |
| When is the last bus? | **O której jest ostatni autobus?**<br>[ɔ 'kturɛj 'jɛst ɔ'statɲi aw'tɔbus?] |
| stop | **przystanek**<br>[pʃi'stanɛk] |

next stop

**następny przystanek**
[na'stɛmpnɨ pʃi'stanɛk]

last stop (terminus)

**ostatni przystanek**
[ɔ'statɲi pʃi'stanɛk]

Stop here, please.

**Proszę się tu zatrzymać.**
['prɔʃɛ ɕiɛ tu za'tʃimatɕ]

Excuse me, this is my stop.

**Przepraszam, to mój przystanek.**
[pʃɛ'praʃam, tɔ muj pʃi'stanɛk]

# Train

| | |
|---|---|
| train | **pociąg**<br>['pɔtɕiɔŋk] |
| suburban train | **kolejka**<br>[kɔ'lɛjka] |
| long-distance train | **pociąg dalekobieżny**<br>['pɔtɕiɔŋk dalɛkɔ'biɛʒni] |
| train station | **dworzec kolejowy**<br>['dvɔʒɛts kɔlɛ'jɔvi] |
| Excuse me, where is the exit to the platform? | **Przepraszam, gdzie jest wyjście z peronu?**<br>[pʃɛ'praʃam, gdʑɛ 'jɛsd 'vijɕtɕɛ s pɛ'rɔnu?] |

| | |
|---|---|
| Does this train go to ...? | **Czy ten pociąg jedzie do ...?**<br>[tʃi 'tɛn 'pɔtɕiɔŋk 'jɛdʑɛ dɔ ...?] |
| next train | **następny pociąg**<br>[na'stɛmpni 'pɔtɕiɔŋk] |
| When is the next train? | **O której jest następny pociąg?**<br>[ɔ 'kturɛj 'jɛst na'stɛmpni 'pɔtɕiɔŋk?] |
| Where can I see the schedule? | **Gdzie znajdę rozkład jazdy?**<br>[gdʑɛ 'znajdɛ 'rɔskwat 'jazdi?] |
| From which platform? | **Z którego peronu?**<br>[s ktu'rɛgɔ pɛ'rɔnu?] |
| When does the train arrive in ...? | **O której ten pociąg dojeżdża do ...?**<br>[ɔ 'kturɛj 'tɛn 'pɔtɕiɔŋk dɔ'jɛʒdʒa dɔ ...?] |

| | |
|---|---|
| Please help me. | **Proszę mi pomóc.**<br>['prɔʃɛ mʲi 'pɔmuts] |
| I'm looking for my seat. | **Szukam swojego miejsca.**<br>['ʃukam sfɔ'jɛgɔ 'mʲɛjstsa] |
| We're looking for our seats. | **Szukamy naszych miejsc.**<br>[ʃu'kami 'naʃix 'mʲɛjsts] |
| My seat is taken. | **Moje miejsce jest zajęte.**<br>['mɔjɛ 'mʲɛjstsɛ 'jɛsd za'jɛntɛ] |
| Our seats are taken. | **Nasze miejsca są zajęte.**<br>['naʃɛ 'mʲɛjstsa 'sɔ̃ za'jɛntɛ] |

| | |
|---|---|
| I'm sorry but this is my seat. | **Przykro mi ale to moje miejsce.**<br>['pʃikrɔ mʲi 'alɛ tɔ 'mɔjɛ 'mʲɛjstsɛ] |
| Is this seat taken? | **Czy to miejsce jest zajęte?**<br>[tʃi tɔ 'mʲɛjstsɛ 'jɛsd za'jɛntɛ?] |
| May I sit here? | **Czy mogę tu usiąść?**<br>[tʃi 'mɔgɛ tu 'uɕiɔ̃ɕtɕ?] |

## On the train. Dialogue (No ticket)

Ticket, please.

**Bilety, proszę.**
[bʲi'lɛti, 'prɔʃɛ]

I don't have a ticket.

**Nie mam biletu.**
[ɲɛ 'mam bʲi'lɛtu]

I lost my ticket.

**Zgubiłem bilet.**
[zgu'bʲiwɛm 'bʲilɛt]

I forgot my ticket at home.

**Zostawiłem bilet w domu.**
[zɔsta'vʲiwɛm 'bʲilɛt v 'dɔmu]

You can buy a ticket from me.

**Może pan /pani/ kupić bilet ode mnie.**
['mɔʒɛ pan /'paɲi/ 'kupʲitɕ 'bʲilɛt 'ɔdɛ 'mɲɛ]

You will also have to pay a fine.

**Będzie pan musiał /pani musiała/ również zapłacić mandat.**
['bɛndʑɛ pan 'muɕaw /'paɲi mu'ɕawa/ 'ruvɲɛʒ za'pwatɕitɕ 'mandat]

Okay.

**Dobrze.**
['dɔbʒɛ]

Where are you going?

**Dokąd pan /pani/ jedzie?**
['dɔkɔnt pan /'paɲi/ 'jɛdʑɛ?]

I'm going to ...

**Jadę do ...**
['jadɛ dɔ ...]

How much? I don't understand.

**Ile kosztuje? Nie rozumiem.**
['ilɛ kɔ'ʃtujɛ? ɲɛ rɔ'zumʲɛm]

Write it down, please.

**Czy może pan /pani/ to napisać?**
[tʃi 'mɔʒɛ pan /'paɲi/ tɔ na'pʲisatɕ?]

Okay. Can I pay with a credit card?

**Dobrze. Czy mogę zapłacić kartą?**
['dɔbʒɛ. tʃi 'mɔgɛ za'pwatɕitɕ 'kartɔ?]

Yes, you can.

**Tak, można.**
[tak, 'mɔʒna]

Here's your receipt.

**Oto pański /pani/ rachunek.**
['ɔtɔ 'paɲskʲi /'paɲi/ ra'xunɛk]

Sorry about the fine.

**Przykro mi z powodu mandatu.**
['pʃikrɔ mʲi s pɔ'vɔdu ma'ndatu]

That's okay. It was my fault.

**W porządku. To moja wina.**
[f pɔ'ʒɔntku. tɔ 'mɔja 'vʲina]

Enjoy your trip.

**Miłej podróży.**
['mʲiwɛj pɔ'druʒi]

# Taxi

| | |
|---|---|
| taxi | **taksówka**<br>[ta'ksufka] |
| taxi driver | **taksówkarz**<br>[ta'ksufkaʃ] |
| to catch a taxi | **złapać taksówkę**<br>['zwapatɕ ta'ksufkɛ] |
| taxi stand | **postój taksówek**<br>['pɔstuj ta'ksuvɛk] |
| Where can I get a taxi? | **Gdzie mogę wziąć taksówkę?**<br>[gdʑɛ 'mɔgɛ vʑi'ɔtɕ ta'ksufkɛ?] |

| | |
|---|---|
| to call a taxi | **zadzwonić po taksówkę**<br>[za'dzvɔɲitɕ pɔ ta'ksufkɛ] |
| I need a taxi. | **Potrzebuję taksówkę.**<br>[pɔtʃɛ'bujɛ ta'ksufkɛ] |
| Right now. | **Jak najszybciej.**<br>['jak na'jʃiptɕɛj] |
| What is your address (location)? | **Skąd pana /panią/ odebrać?**<br>['skɔnt 'pana /'paɲiɔ̃/ ɔ'dɛbratɕ?] |
| My address is ... | **Mój adres to ...**<br>[muj 'adrɛs tɔ ...] |
| Your destination? | **Dokąd pan /pani/ chce jechać?**<br>['dɔkɔnt pa'n /paɲi/ 'xtsɛ 'jɛxatɕ?] |

| | |
|---|---|
| Excuse me, ... | **Przepraszam, ...**<br>[pʃɛ'praʃam, ...] |
| Are you available? | **Czy jest pan wolny?**<br>[tʃi 'jɛst pan 'vɔlni?] |
| How much is it to get to ...? | **Ile kosztuje przejazd do ...?**<br>['ilɛ kɔ'ʃtujɛ 'pʃɛjazd dɔ ...?] |
| Do you know where it is? | **Wie pan /pani/ gdzie to jest?**<br>['vʲɛ pan /'paɲi/ gdʑɛ tɔ 'jɛst?] |
| Airport, please. | **Na lotnisko, proszę.**<br>[na lɔt'ɲiskɔ, 'prɔʃɛ] |
| Stop here, please. | **Proszę się tu zatrzymać.**<br>['prɔʃɛ ɕɛ tu za'tʃimatɕ] |
| It's not here. | **To nie tutaj.**<br>[tɔ ɲɛ 'tutaj] |
| This is the wrong address. | **To zły adres.**<br>[tɔ 'zwi 'adrɛs] |
| Turn left. | **Proszę skręcić w lewo.**<br>['prɔʃɛ 'skrɛntɕitɕ v 'lɛvɔ] |
| Turn right. | **Proszę skręcić w prawo.**<br>['prɔʃɛ 'skrɛntɕitɕ f 'pravɔ] |

| | |
|---|---|
| How much do I owe you? | **Ile płacę?**<br>['ilɛ 'pwatsɛ?] |
| I'd like a receipt, please. | **Poproszę rachunek.**<br>[pɔ'prɔʃɛ ra'xunɛk] |
| Keep the change. | **Proszę zachować resztę.**<br>['prɔʃɛ za'xɔvatɕ 'rɛʃtɛ] |
| Would you please wait for me? | **Czy może pan /pani/<br>na mnie poczekać?**<br>[tʃi 'mɔʒɛ pan /'paɲi/<br>na mɲɛ pɔ'tʃɛkatɕ?] |
| five minutes | **pięć minut**<br>['pʲiɛntɕ 'mʲinut] |
| ten minutes | **dziesięć minut**<br>['dʑɛɕiɛntɕ 'mʲinut] |
| fifteen minutes | **piętnaście minut**<br>[pʲiɛ'ntnaɕtɕɛ 'mʲinut] |
| twenty minutes | **dwadzieścia minut**<br>[dva'dʑɛɕtɕa 'mʲinut] |
| half an hour | **pół godziny**<br>['puw gɔ'dʑini] |

# Hotel

Hello.
**Witam.**
['vitam]

My name is …
**Mam na imię …**
[mam na 'imiɛ …]

I have a reservation.
**Mam rezerwację.**
[mam rɛzɛ'rvatsjɛ]

I need …
**Potrzebuję …**
[pɔtʃɛ'bujɛ …]

a single room
**pojedynczy pokój**
[pɔjɛ'diɳtʃi 'pɔkuj]

a double room
**podwójny pokój**
[pɔ'dvujni 'pɔkuj]

How much is that?
**Ile to kosztuje?**
['ilɛ tɔ kɔ'ʃtujɛ?]

That's a bit expensive.
**To trochę za drogo.**
[tɔ 'trɔxɛ za 'drɔgɔ]

Do you have any other options?
**Czy są inne pokoje?**
[tʃi 'sõ 'innɛ pɔ'kɔjɛ?]

I'll take it.
**Wezmę ten.**
['vɛzmɛ 'tɛn]

I'll pay in cash.
**Zapłacę gotówką.**
[za'pwatsɛ gɔ'tufkõ]

I've got a problem.
**Mam problem.**
[mam 'prɔblɛm]

My … is broken.
**… jest zepsuty /zepsuta/.**
[… 'jɛsd zɛ'psuti /zɛ'psuta/.]

My … is out of order.
**… jest nieczynny /nieczynna/.**
[… 'jɛst ɲɛ'tʃinni /ɲɛ'tʃinna/.]

TV
**Mój telewizor …**
[muj tɛlɛ'vizɔr …]

air conditioning
**Moja klimatyzacja …**
['mɔja kʎimati'zatsja …]

tap
**Mój kran …**
[muj 'kran …]

shower
**Mój prysznic …**
[muj 'priʃnits …]

sink
**Mój zlew …**
[muj 'zlɛf …]

safe
**Mój sejf …**
[muj 'sɛjf …]

| | |
|---|---|
| door lock | **Mój zamek ...**<br>[muj 'zamɛk ...] |
| electrical outlet | **Moje gniazdko elektryczne ...**<br>['mɔjɛ 'gɲaztkɔ ɛlɛ'ktritʃnɛ ...] |
| hairdryer | **Moja suszarka ...**<br>['mɔja su'ʃarka ...] |

| | |
|---|---|
| I don't have ... | **Nie mam ...**<br>[ɲɛ 'mam ...] |
| water | **wody**<br>['vɔdɨ] |
| light | **światła**<br>['ɕviatwa] |
| electricity | **prądu**<br>['prɔndu] |

| | |
|---|---|
| Can you give me ...? | **Czy może mi pan /pani/ przynieść ...?**<br>[tʃɨ 'mɔʒɛ mʲi pan /'paɲi/ 'pʃɨɲɛɕtɕ ...?] |
| a towel | **ręcznik**<br>['rɛntʃɲik] |
| a blanket | **koc**<br>['kɔts] |
| slippers | **kapcie**<br>['kaptɕɛ] |
| a robe | **szlafrok**<br>['ʃlafrɔk] |
| shampoo | **szampon**<br>['ʃampɔn] |
| soap | **mydło**<br>['mɨdwɔ] |

| | |
|---|---|
| I'd like to change rooms. | **Chciałbym /chciałabym/ zmienić pokój.**<br>['xtɕawbɨm /xtɕa'wabɨm/ 'zmʲɛɲitɕ 'pɔkuj] |
| I can't find my key. | **Nie mogę znaleźć mojego klucza.**<br>[ɲɛ 'mɔgɛ 'znalɛɕtɕ mɔ'jɛgɔ 'klutʃa] |
| Could you open my room, please? | **Czy może pani otworzyć mój pokój?**<br>[tʃɨ 'mɔʒɛ 'paɲi ɔ'tfɔʒɨtɕ muj 'pɔkuj?] |
| Who's there? | **Kto tam?**<br>[ktɔ tam?] |
| Come in! | **Proszę wejść!**<br>['prɔʃɛ 'vɛjɕtɕ!] |
| Just a minute! | **Chwileczkę!**<br>[xvʲi'lɛtʃkɛ!] |
| Not right now, please. | **Nie teraz, proszę.**<br>[ɲɛ 'tɛras, 'prɔʃɛ] |

| | |
|---|---|
| Come to my room, please. | **Proszę wejść do mojego pokoju.**<br>['prɔʃɛ 'vɛjɕtɕ dɔ mɔ'jɛgɔ pɔ'kɔju] |
| My room number is ... | **Mój numer pokoju to ...**<br>[muj 'numɛr pɔ'kɔju tɔ ...] |

I'd like to order food service.

**Chciałbym /chciałabym/ zamówić posiłek do pokoju.**
['xtɕawbim /xtɕa'wabim/ za'muvʲitɕ pɔ'ɕiwɛg dɔ pɔ'kɔju]

I'm leaving ...

**Wyjeżdżam ...**
[vɨ'jɛʒdʒam ...]

We're leaving ...

**Wyjeżdżamy ...**
[vɨjɛ'ʒdʒamɨ ...]

right now

**jak najszybciej**
['jak na'jʂiptɕɛj]

this afternoon

**po południu**
[pɔ pɔ'wudɲu]

tonight

**dziś wieczorem**
['dʑiɕ vʲɛ'tʂɔrɛm]

tomorrow

**jutro**
['jutrɔ]

tomorrow morning

**jutro rano**
['jutrɔ 'ranɔ]

tomorrow evening

**jutro wieczorem**
['jutrɔ vʲɛ'tʂɔrɛm]

the day after tomorrow

**pojutrze**
[pɔ'jutʂɛ]

I'd like to pay.

**Chciałbym zapłacić.**
['xtɕawbim za'pwatɕitɕ]

Everything was wonderful.

**Wszystko było wspaniałe.**
[fʂistkɔ 'biwɔ fspa'ɲawɛ]

Where can I get a taxi?

**Gdzie mogę wziąć taksówkę?**
[gdʑɛ 'mɔgɛ vʑi'ɔtɕ ta'ksufkɛ?]

Would you call a taxi for me, please?

**Czy może pan /pani/ wezwać dla mnie taksówkę?**
[tʂɨ 'mɔʒɛ pan /'paɲi/ 'vɛzvatɕ 'dla 'mɲɛ ta'ksufkɛ?]

# Restaurant

Can I look at the menu, please? | **Czy mogę prosić menu?**
[ʧi 'mɔgɛ 'prɔɕiʨ 'mɛnu?]

Table for one. | **Stolik dla jednej osoby.**
['stɔʎig 'dla 'jɛdnɛj ɔ'sɔbi]

There are two (three, four) of us. | **Jest nas dwoje (troje, czworo).**
['jɛst 'naz 'dvɔjɛ ('trɔjɛ, 'ʧvɔrɔ)]

Smoking | **Dla palących.**
['dla pa'lɔntsix]

No smoking | **Dla niepalących.**
['dla ɲɛpa'lɔntsix]

Excuse me! (addressing a waiter) | **Przepraszam!**
[pʃɛ'praʃam!]

menu | **menu**
['mɛnu]

wine list | **lista win**
['ʎista 'vʲin]

The menu, please. | **Poproszę menu.**
[pɔ'prɔʃɛ 'mɛnu]

Are you ready to order? | **Czy są Państwo gotowi?**
[ʧi 'sɔ̃ 'paɲstfɔ gɔ'tɔvʲi?]

What will you have? | **Co Państwo zamawiają?**
['tsɔ 'paɲstfɔ zama'vʲajɔ̃?]

I'll have … | **Zamawiam …**
[za'mavʲam …]

I'm a vegetarian. | **Jestem wegetarianinem /wegetarianką/.**
['jɛstɛm vɛgɛtaria'ɲinɛm /vɛgɛta'riankɔ̃/]

meat | **mięso**
['mʲiɛ̃sɔ]

fish | **ryba**
['riba]

vegetables | **warzywa**
[va'ʒiva]

Do you have vegetarian dishes? | **Czy są dania wegetariańskie?**
[ʧi 'sɔ̃ 'daɲa vɛgɛta'riaɲskʲɛ?]

I don't eat pork. | **Nie jadam wieprzowiny.**
[ɲɛ 'jadam vʲɛpʃɔ'vʲini]

He /she/ doesn't eat meat. | **On /Ona/ nie je mięsa.**
[ɔn /'ɔna/ ɲɛ 'jɛ 'mʲiɛ̃sa]

I am allergic to ...

**Jestem uczulony /uczulona/ na ...**
['jɛstɛm utʃu'lɔni /utʃu'lɔna/ na ...]

Would you please bring me ...

**Czy może pan /pani/ przynieść mi ...**
[tʃi 'mɔʒɛ pan /'paɲi/ 'pʃiɲɛɕtɕ mʲi ...]

salt | pepper | sugar

**sól | pieprz | cukier**
['suʌ | 'pʲɛpʃ | 'tsukʲɛr]

coffee | tea | dessert

**kawa | herbata | deser**
['kava | xɛ'rbata | 'dɛsɛr]

water | sparkling | plain

**woda | gazowana | bez gazu**
['vɔda | gazɔ'vana | 'bɛz 'gazu]

a spoon | fork | knife

**łyżka | widelec | nóż**
['wiʃka | vʲi'dɛlɛts | 'nuʒ]

a plate | napkin

**talerz | serwetka**
['talɛʃ | sɛr'vɛtka]

Enjoy your meal!

**Smacznego!**
[sma'tʃnɛgɔ!]

One more, please.

**Jeszcze raz poproszę.**
['jɛʃtʃɛ 'ras pɔ'prɔʃɛ]

It was very delicious.

**To było pyszne.**
[tɔ 'biwɔ 'piʃnɛ]

check | change | tip

**rachunek | drobne | napiwek**
[ra'xunɛk | 'drɔbnɛ | na'pʲivɛk]

Check, please.
(Could I have the check, please?)

**Rachunek proszę.**
[ra'xunɛk 'prɔʃɛ]

Can I pay by credit card?

**Czy mogę zapłacić kartą?**
[tʃi 'mɔgɛ za'pwatɕitɕ 'kartɔ̃?]

I'm sorry, there's a mistake here.

**Przykro mi, tu jest błąd.**
['pʃikrɔ mʲi, tu 'jɛsd 'bwɔnt]

# Shopping

| | |
|---|---|
| Can I help you? | **W czym mogę pomóc?**<br>[f 'ʧim 'mɔgɛ 'pɔmuts?] |
| Do you have ...? | **Czy jest ...?**<br>[ʧi 'jɛst ...?] |
| I'm looking for ... | **Szukam ...**<br>['ʃukam ...] |
| I need ... | **Potrzebuję ...**<br>[pɔʧɛ'bujɛ ...] |

| | |
|---|---|
| I'm just looking. | **Tylko się rozglądam.**<br>['tɨlkɔ ɕɛ rɔ'zglɔndam] |
| We're just looking. | **Tylko się rozglądamy.**<br>['tɨlkɔ ɕɛ rɔzglɔn'damɨ] |
| I'll come back later. | **Wrócę później.**<br>['vrutsɛ 'puʑɲɛj] |
| We'll come back later. | **Wrócimy później.**<br>[vru'ʧimɨ 'puʑɲɛj] |
| discounts \| sale | **zniżka \| wyprzedaż**<br>['zɲiʃka \| vi'pʃɛdaʒ] |

| | |
|---|---|
| Would you please show me ... | **Czy może mi pan /pani/ pokazać ...**<br>[ʧi 'mɔʒɛ mʲi pan /'paɲi/ pɔ'kazaʨ ...] |
| Would you please give me ... | **Czy może mi pan /pani/ dać ...**<br>[ʧi 'mɔʒɛ mʲi pan /'paɲi/ daʨ ...] |
| Can I try it on? | **Czy mogę przymierzyć?**<br>[ʧi 'mɔgɛ pʃi'mʲɛʒiʨ?] |
| Excuse me, where's the fitting room? | **Przepraszam,<br>gdzie jest przymierzalnia?**<br>[pʃɛ'praʃam,<br>gdʑɛ 'jɛst pʃimʲɛ'ʒalɲa?] |
| Which color would you like? | **Jaki kolor pan /pani/ sobie życzy?**<br>['jakʲi 'kɔlɔr pan /'paɲi/ 'sɔbʲɛ 'ʒiʧi?] |
| size \| length | **rozmiar \| długość**<br>['rɔzmʲar \| 'dwugɔɕʨ] |
| How does it fit? | **Jak to leży?**<br>['jak tɔ 'lɛʒi?] |

| | |
|---|---|
| How much is it? | **Ile to kosztuje?**<br>['ilɛ tɔ kɔ'ʃtujɛ?] |
| That's too expensive. | **To za drogo.**<br>[tɔ za 'drɔgɔ] |
| I'll take it. | **Wezmę to.**<br>['vɛzmɛ 'tɔ] |

Excuse me, where do I pay?

**Przepraszam, gdzie mogę zapłacić?**
[pʃɛ'praʃam, gdʑɛ 'mɔgɛ za'pwatɕitɕ?]

Will you pay in cash or credit card?

**Czy płaci pan /pani/ gotówką czy kartą?**
[ʧi 'pwatɕi pan /'paɲi/ gɔ'tufkɔ̃ ʧi 'kartɔ̃?]

In cash | with credit card

**Gotówką | kartą kredytową**
[gɔ'tufkɔ̃ | 'kartɔ̃ krɛdi'tɔvɔ̃]

Do you want the receipt?

**Czy chce pan /pani/ rachunek?**
[ʧi xtsɛ pan /'paɲi/ ra'xunɛk?]

Yes, please.

**Tak, proszę.**
[tak, 'prɔʃɛ]

No, it's OK.

**Nie, dziękuję.**
[ɲɛ, dʑɛ'ŋkujɛ]

Thank you. Have a nice day!

**Dziękuję. Miłego dnia!**
[dʑɛŋ'kujɛ. mʲi'wɛgɔ dɲa!]

# In town

| | |
|---|---|
| Excuse me, please. | **Przepraszam.**<br>[pʃɛ'praʃam] |
| I'm looking for ... | **Szukam ...**<br>['ʃukam ...] |
| the subway | **metra**<br>['mɛtra] |
| my hotel | **mojego hotelu**<br>[mɔ'jɛgɔ xɔ'tɛlu] |
| the movie theater | **kina**<br>['kʲina] |
| a taxi stand | **postoju taksówek**<br>[pɔ'stɔju ta'ksuvɛk] |
| an ATM | **bankomatu**<br>[bankɔ'matu] |
| a foreign exchange office | **kantoru wymiany walut**<br>[ka'ntɔru viˈmʲani vaˈlut] |
| an internet café | **kafejki internetowej**<br>[kaˈfɛjkʲi intɛrnɛ'tɔvɛj] |
| ... street | **ulicy ...**<br>[uˈʎitsi ...] |
| this place | **tego miejsca**<br>['tɛgɔ 'mʲɛjstsa] |
| Do you know where ... is? | **Czy wie pan /pani/ gdzie jest ...?**<br>[tʃi 'vʲɛ pan /'paɲi/ gdʑɛ 'jɛst ...?] |
| Which street is this? | **Na jakiej to ulicy?**<br>[na 'jakʲɛj tɔ uˈʎitsi?] |
| Show me where we are right now. | **Proszę mi pokazać<br>gdzie teraz jesteśmy.**<br>['prɔʃɛ mʲi pɔ'kazatɕ<br>gdʑɛ 'tɛras jɛ'stɛɕmi] |
| Can I get there on foot? | **Czy mogę tam dojść pieszo?**<br>[tʃi 'mɔgɛ tam 'dɔjɕtɕ 'pʲɛʃɔ?] |
| Do you have a map of the city? | **Czy ma pan /pani/ mapę miasta?**<br>[tʃi ma pan /'paɲi/ 'mapɛ 'mʲasta?] |
| How much is a ticket to get in? | **Ile kosztuje wejście?**<br>['ilɛ kɔ'ʃtujɛ 'vɛjɕtɕɛ?] |
| Can I take pictures here? | **Czy można tu robić zdjęcia?**<br>[tʃi 'mɔʒna tu 'rɔbʲitɕ 'zdjɛntɕa?] |
| Are you open? | **Czy jest otwarte?**<br>[tʃi 'jɛst ɔ'tfartɛ?] |

When do you open?

**Od której jest czynne?**
[ɔt 'kturɛj 'jɛst 'ʧinnɛ?]

When do you close?

**Do której jest czynne?**
[dɔ 'kturɛj 'jɛst 'ʧinnɛ?]

# Money

| | |
|---|---|
| money | **pieniądze**<br>[pʲɛ'ɲiɔndzɛ] |
| cash | **gotówka**<br>[gɔ'tufka] |
| paper money | **pieniądze papierowe**<br>[pʲɛ'ɲiɔndzɛ papʲɛ'rɔvɛ] |
| loose change | **drobne**<br>['drɔbnɛ] |
| check \| change \| tip | **rachunek \| drobne \| napiwek**<br>[ra'xunɛk \| 'drɔbnɛ \| na'pʲivɛk] |

| | |
|---|---|
| credit card | **karta kredytowa**<br>['karta krɛdɨ'tɔva] |
| wallet | **portfel**<br>['pɔrtfɛl] |
| to buy | **kupować**<br>[ku'pɔvatɕ] |
| to pay | **płacić**<br>['pwatɕitɕ] |
| fine | **grzywna**<br>['gʒɨvna] |
| free | **darmowy**<br>[da'rmɔvɨ] |

| | |
|---|---|
| Where can I buy ...? | **Gdzie mogę kupić ...?**<br>[gdʑɛ 'mɔgɛ 'kupʲitɕ ...?] |
| Is the bank open now? | **Czy bank jest teraz otwarty?**<br>[ʧɨ 'bank 'jɛst 'tɛraz ɔ'tfarti?] |
| When does it open? | **Od której jest czynny?**<br>[ɔt 'kturɛj 'jɛst 'ʧinni?] |
| When does it close? | **Do której jest czynny?**<br>[dɔ 'kturɛj 'jɛst 'ʧinni?] |

| | |
|---|---|
| How much? | **Ile kosztuje?**<br>['ilɛ kɔ'ʃtujɛ?] |
| How much is this? | **Ile to kosztuje?**<br>['ilɛ tɔ kɔ'ʃtujɛ?] |
| That's too expensive. | **To za drogo.**<br>[tɔ za 'drɔgɔ] |

| | |
|---|---|
| Excuse me, where do I pay? | **Przepraszam, gdzie mogę zapłacić?**<br>[pʃɛ'praʃam, gdʑɛ 'mɔgɛ za'pwatɕitɕ?] |
| Check, please. | **Rachunek proszę.**<br>[ra'xunɛk 'prɔʃɛ] |

Can I pay by credit card?

**Czy mogę zapłacić kartą?**
[tʃi 'mɔgɛ za'pwatɕitɕ 'kartɔ̃?]

Is there an ATM here?

**Czy jest tu gdzieś bankomat?**
[tʃi 'jɛst tu gdʑɛɕ bankɔ'mat?]

I'm looking for an ATM.

**Szukam bankomatu.**
['ʃukam bankɔ'matu]

I'm looking for a foreign exchange office.

**Szukam kantoru wymiany walut.**
['ʃukam ka'ntɔru vi'mʲani 'valut]

I'd like to change ...

**Chciałbym /Chciałabym/ wymienić ...**
['xtɕawbim /xtɕa'wabim/ vi'mʲɛɲitɕ ...]

What is the exchange rate?

**Jaki jest kurs?**
['jakʲi 'jɛst 'kurs?]

Do you need my passport?

**Czy potrzebuje pan /pani/ mój paszport?**
[tʃi pɔtʃɛ'bujɛ pan /'paɲi/ muj 'paʃport?]

# Time

| | |
|---|---|
| What time is it? | **Która godzina?**<br>['ktura gɔ'dzina?] |
| When? | **Kiedy?**<br>['kʲɛdʲ?] |
| At what time? | **O której godzinie?**<br>[ɔ 'kturɛj gɔ'dziɲɛ?] |
| now \| later \| after … | **teraz \| później \| po …**<br>['tɛraz \| 'puzɲɛj \| pɔ …] |
| one o'clock | **godzina pierwsza**<br>[gɔ'dzina 'pʲɛrʃʃa] |
| one fifteen | **pierwsza piętnaście**<br>['pʲɛrʃʃa pʲɛ'ntnaɕtɕɛ] |
| one thirty | **pierwsza trzydzieści**<br>['pʲɛrʃʃa ʧi'dzɛɕtɕi] |
| one forty-five | **za piętnaście druga**<br>[za pʲɛ'ntnaɕtɕɛ 'druga] |
| one \| two \| three | **pierwsza \| druga \| trzecia**<br>['pʲɛrʃʃa \| 'druga \| 'ʧɛtɕa] |
| four \| five \| six | **czwarta \| piąta \| szósta**<br>['ʧvarta \| 'pʲiɔnta \| 'ʃusta] |
| seven \| eight \| nine | **siódma \| ósma \| dziewiąta**<br>['ɕudma \| 'usma \| dzɛ'vʲiɔnta] |
| ten \| eleven \| twelve | **dziesiąta \| jedenasta \| dwunasta**<br>[dzɛ'ɕiɔnta \| jɛdɛ'nasta \| dvu'nasta] |
| in … | **za …**<br>[za …] |
| five minutes | **pięć minut**<br>['pʲiɛntɕ 'mʲinut] |
| ten minutes | **dziesięć minut**<br>['dzɛɕiɛntɕ 'mʲinut] |
| fifteen minutes | **piętnaście minut**<br>[pʲɛ'ntnaɕtɕɛ 'mʲinut] |
| twenty minutes | **dwadzieścia minut**<br>[dva'dzɛɕtɕa 'mʲinut] |
| half an hour | **pół godziny**<br>['puw gɔ'dzini] |
| an hour | **godzinę**<br>[gɔ'dziɲɛ] |

| | |
|---|---|
| in the morning | **rano**<br>['ranɔ] |
| early in the morning | **wcześnie rano**<br>['ftʃɛɕɲɛ 'ranɔ] |
| this morning | **tego ranka**<br>['tɛgɔ 'ranka] |
| tomorrow morning | **jutro rano**<br>['jutrɔ 'ranɔ] |
| at noon | **w południe**<br>[f pɔ'wudɲɛ] |
| in the afternoon | **po południu**<br>[pɔ pɔ'wudɲu] |
| in the evening | **wieczorem**<br>[vʲɛ'tʃɔrɛm] |
| tonight | **dziś wieczorem**<br>['dʑiɕ vʲɛ'tʃɔrɛm] |
| at night | **w nocy**<br>[f 'nɔtsɨ] |
| yesterday | **wczoraj**<br>['ftʃɔraj] |
| today | **dzisiaj**<br>['dʑiɕaj] |
| tomorrow | **jutro**<br>['jutrɔ] |
| the day after tomorrow | **pojutrze**<br>[pɔ'jutʃɛ] |
| What day is it today? | **Jaki jest dzisiaj dzień?**<br>['jakʲi 'jɛst 'dʑiɕaj 'dʑɛɲ?] |
| It's ... | **Jest ...**<br>['jɛst ...] |
| Monday | **poniedziałek**<br>[pɔɲɛ'dʑawɛk] |
| Tuesday | **wtorek**<br>['ftɔrɛk] |
| Wednesday | **środa**<br>['ɕrɔda] |
| Thursday | **czwartek**<br>['tʃvartɛk] |
| Friday | **piątek**<br>['pʲiɔntɛk] |
| Saturday | **sobota**<br>[sɔ'bɔta] |
| Sunday | **niedziela**<br>[ɲɛ'dʑɛla] |

# Greetings. Introductions

Hello.

**Witam.**
['vʲitam]

Pleased to meet you.

**Miło mi pana /panią/ poznać.**
['mʲiwɔ mʲi 'pana /'paɲiɔ̃/ 'pɔznatɕ]

Me too.

**Mi również.**
[mʲi 'ruvɲɛʒ]

I'd like you to meet ...

**Chciałbym żeby pan poznał /pani poznała/ ...**
['xtɕawbim 'ʒɛbi pan 'pɔznaw /'paɲi pɔ'znawa/ ...]

Nice to meet you.

**Miło pana /panią/ poznać.**
['mʲiwɔ 'pana /'paɲiɔ̃/ 'pɔznatɕ]

How are you?

**Jak się pan /pani/ miewa?**
['jak ɕɛ pan /'paɲi/ 'mʲɛva?]

My name is ...

**Mam na imię ...**
[mam na 'imʲiɛ ...]

His name is ...

**On ma na imię ...**
['ɔn ma na 'imʲiɛ ...]

Her name is ...

**Ona ma na imię ...**
['ɔna ma na 'imʲiɛ ...]

What's your name?

**Jak pan /pani/ ma na imię?**
['jak pan /'paɲi/ ma na 'imʲiɛ?]

What's his name?

**Jak on ma na imię?**
['jak 'ɔn ma na 'imʲiɛ?]

What's her name?

**Jak ona ma na imię?**
['jak 'ɔna ma na 'imʲiɛ?]

What's your last name?

**Jak pan /pani/ się nazywa?**
['jak pan /'paɲi/ ɕɛ na'ziva?]

You can call me ...

**Może się pan /pani/ do mnie zwracać ...**
['mɔʒɛ ɕɛ pa'n /paɲi/ dɔ 'mɲɛ 'zvratsatɕ ...]

Where are you from?

**Skąd pan /pani/ jest?**
['skɔnt pan /'paɲi/ 'jɛst?]

I'm from ...

**Pochodzę z ...**
[pɔ'xɔdzɛ s ...]

What do you do for a living?

**Czym się pan /pani/ zajmuje?**
['tʃim ɕɛ pan /'paɲi/ zaj'mujɛ?]

Who is this?

**Kto to jest?**
[ktɔ tɔ 'jɛst?]

Who is he?

**Kim on jest?**
['kʲim 'ɔn 'jɛst?]

| | |
|---|---|
| Who is she? | **Kim ona jest?** |
| | ['kⁱim 'ɔna 'jɛst?] |
| Who are they? | **Kim oni są?** |
| | ['kⁱim 'ɔɲi sɔ̃?] |

| | |
|---|---|
| This is ... | **To jest ...** |
| | [tɔ 'jɛst ...] |
| my friend (masc.) | **mój przyjaciel** |
| | [muj pʃiˈjatɕɛl] |
| my friend (fem.) | **moja przyjaciółka** |
| | ['mɔja pʃijaˈtɕuwka] |
| my husband | **mój mąż** |
| | [muj 'mɔ̃ʒ] |
| my wife | **moja żona** |
| | ['mɔja 'ʒɔna] |

| | |
|---|---|
| my father | **mój ojciec** |
| | [muj 'ɔjtɕɛts] |
| my mother | **moja matka** |
| | ['mɔja 'matka] |
| my brother | **mój brat** |
| | [muj 'brat] |
| my sister | **moja siostra** |
| | ['mɔja 'ɕɔstra] |
| my son | **mój syn** |
| | [muj 'sin] |
| my daughter | **moja córka** |
| | ['mɔja 'tsurka] |

| | |
|---|---|
| This is our son. | **To jest nasz syn.** |
| | [tɔ 'jɛst 'naʃ 'sin] |
| This is our daughter. | **To jest nasza córka.** |
| | [tɔ 'jɛst 'naʃa 'tsurka] |
| These are my children. | **To moje dzieci.** |
| | [tɔ 'mɔjɛ 'dʑɛtɕi] |
| These are our children. | **To nasze dzieci.** |
| | [tɔ 'naʃɛ 'dʑɛtɕi] |

# Farewells

| Good bye! | **Do widzenia!**<br>[dɔ vʲi'dzɛɲa!] |
|---|---|
| Bye! (inform.) | **Cześć!**<br>['ʧɛɕʨ!] |
| See you tomorrow. | **Do zobaczenia jutro.**<br>[dɔ zɔba'ʧɛɲa 'jutrɔ] |
| See you soon. | **Na razie.**<br>[na 'razɛ] |
| See you at seven. | **Do zobaczenia o siódmej.**<br>[dɔ zɔba'ʧɛɲa ɔ 'ɕudmɛj] |

| Have fun! | **Bawcie się dobrze!**<br>['baftɕɛ ɕiɛ 'dɔbʒɛ!] |
|---|---|
| Talk to you later. | **Do usłyszenia.**<br>[dɔ uswɨ'ʃɛɲa] |
| Have a nice weekend. | **Miłego weekendu.**<br>[mʲi'wɛgɔ vɛɛ'kɛndu] |
| Good night. | **Dobranoc.**<br>[dɔ'branɔts] |

| It's time for me to go. | **Czas na mnie.**<br>[ʧas na 'mɲɛ] |
|---|---|
| I have to go. | **Muszę iść.**<br>['muʃɛ 'iɕʨ] |
| I will be right back. | **Wracam za chwilę.**<br>['vratsam za 'xvʲilɛ] |

| It's late. | **Późno już.**<br>['puʑnɔ 'juʒ] |
|---|---|
| I have to get up early. | **Muszę wstać wcześnie.**<br>['muʃɛ 'fstaʨ 'fʧɛɕɲɛ] |
| I'm leaving tomorrow. | **Wyjeżdżam jutro.**<br>[vɨ'jɛʒdʒam 'jutrɔ] |
| We're leaving tomorrow. | **Wyjeżdżamy jutro.**<br>[vɨjɛʒ'dʒami 'jutrɔ] |

| Have a nice trip! | **Miłej podróży!**<br>['mʲiwɛj pɔ'druʒi!] |
|---|---|
| It was nice meeting you. | **Miło było pana /panią/ poznać.**<br>['mʲiwɔ 'bɨwɔ 'pana /'paɲiɔ̃/ 'pɔznaʨ] |
| It was nice talking to you. | **Miło się rozmawiało.**<br>['mʲiwɔ ɕiɛ rɔzma'vʲawɔ] |
| Thanks for everything. | **Dziękuję za wszystko.**<br>[dʑiɛŋ'kujɛ za 'fʃistkɔ] |

I had a very good time.

**Dobrze się bawiłem /bawiłam/.**
['dɔbʒɛ ɕiɛ ba'vʲiwɛm /ba'vʲiwam/]

We had a very good time.

**Dobrze się bawiliśmy.**
['dɔbʒɛ ɕiɛ bavʲi'ʎiɕmi]

It was really great.

**Było naprawdę świetne.**
['biwɔ na'pravdɛ 'ɕvʲɛtnɛ]

I'm going to miss you.

**Będę tęsknić.**
['bɛndɛ 'tɛ̃skɲitɕ]

We're going to miss you.

**Będziemy tęsknić.**
[bɛ'ndʑɛmi 'tɛ̃skɲitɕ]

Good luck!

**Powodzenia!**
[pɔvɔ'dzɛɲa!]

Say hi to ...

**Pozdrów ...**
['pɔzdruf ...]

# Foreign language

| | |
|---|---|
| I don't understand. | **Nie rozumiem.** <br> [ɲɛ rɔ'zumʲɛm] |
| Write it down, please. | **Czy może pan /pani/ to napisać?** <br> [tʃi 'mɔʒɛ pan /'paɲi/ tɔ na'pʲisatɕ?] |
| Do you speak ...? | **Czy mówi pan /pani/ po ...?** <br> [tʃi 'muvʲi pan /'paɲi/ pɔ ...?] |

| | |
|---|---|
| I speak a little bit of ... | **Mówię troszkę po ...** <br> ['muvʲiɛ 'trɔʃkɛ pɔ ...] |
| English | **angielsku** <br> [a'ŋɡʲɛlsku] |
| Turkish | **turecku** <br> [tu'rɛtsku] |
| Arabic | **arabsku** <br> [a'rapsku] |
| French | **francusku** <br> [fran'tsusku] |

| | |
|---|---|
| German | **niemiecku** <br> [ɲɛ'mʲɛtsku] |
| Italian | **włosku** <br> ['vwɔsku] |
| Spanish | **hiszpańsku** <br> [xi'ʃpaɲsku] |
| Portuguese | **portugalsku** <br> [pɔrtu'ɡalsku] |
| Chinese | **chińsku** <br> ['xiɲsku] |
| Japanese | **japońsku** <br> [ja'pɔɲsku] |

| | |
|---|---|
| Can you repeat that, please. | **Czy może pan /pani/ powtórzyć?** <br> [tʃi 'mɔʒɛ pan /'paɲi/ pɔ'ftuʒitɕ?] |
| I understand. | **Rozumiem.** <br> [rɔ'zumʲɛm] |
| I don't understand. | **Nie rozumiem.** <br> [ɲɛ rɔ'zumʲɛm] |
| Please speak more slowly. | **Proszę mówić wolniej.** <br> ['prɔʃɛ 'muvʲitɕ 'vɔlɲɛj] |

| | |
|---|---|
| Is that correct? (Am I saying it right?) | **Czy jest poprawne?** <br> [tʃi 'jɛst pɔ'pravnɛ?] |
| What is this? (What does this mean?) | **Co to znaczy?** <br> ['tsɔ tɔ 'znatʃi?] |

## Apologies

| | |
|---|---|
| Excuse me, please. | **Przepraszam.**<br>[pʃɛ'praʃam] |
| I'm sorry. | **Przepraszam.**<br>[pʃɛ'praʃam] |
| I'm really sorry. | **Bardzo przepraszam.**<br>['bardzɔ pʃɛ'praʃam] |
| Sorry, it's my fault. | **Przepraszam, to moja wina.**<br>[pʃɛ'praʃam, tɔ 'mɔja 'vʲina] |
| My mistake. | **Mój błąd.**<br>[muj 'bwɔnt] |

| | |
|---|---|
| May I ...? | **Czy mogę ...?**<br>[tʃi 'mɔgɛ ...?] |
| Do you mind if I ...? | **Czy ma pan /pani/<br>coś przeciwko gdybym ...?**<br>[tʃi ma pan /'paɲi/<br>'tsɔɕ pʃɛ'tɕifkɔ 'gdibim ...?] |
| It's OK. | **Nic się nie stało.**<br>['ɲits ɕɛ ɲɛ 'stawɔ] |
| It's all right. | **Wszystko w porządku.**<br>['fʃistkɔ f pɔ'ʒɔntku] |
| Don't worry about it. | **Nic nie szkodzi.**<br>['ɲits ɲɛ 'ʃkɔdʑi] |

# Agreement

| | |
|---|---|
| Yes. | **Tak.**<br>[tak] |
| Yes, sure. | **Tak, oczywiście.**<br>[tak, ɔtʃi'vʲiɕtɕɛ] |
| OK (Good!) | **Dobrze!**<br>['dɔbʒɛ!] |
| Very well. | **Bardzo dobrze.**<br>['bardzɔ 'dɔbʒɛ] |
| Certainly! | **Oczywiście!**<br>[ɔtʃi'vʲiɕtɕɛ!] |
| I agree. | **Zgadzam się.**<br>['zgadzam ɕɛ] |

| | |
|---|---|
| That's correct. | **Dokładnie tak.**<br>[dɔ'kwadɲɛ 'tak] |
| That's right. | **Zgadza się.**<br>['zgadza ɕɛ] |
| You're right. | **Ma pan /pani/ rację.**<br>[ma pan /'paɲi/ 'ratsjɛ] |
| I don't mind. | **Nie mam nic przeciwko.**<br>[ɲɛ 'mam 'ɲits pʃɛ'tɕifkɔ] |
| Absolutely right. | **Bardzo poprawnie.**<br>['bardzɔ pɔ'pravɲɛ] |

| | |
|---|---|
| It's possible. | **To możliwe.**<br>[tɔ mɔ'ʒʎivɛ] |
| That's a good idea. | **To dobry pomysł.**<br>[tɔ 'dɔbri 'pɔmis] |
| I can't say no. | **Nie mogę odmówić.**<br>[ɲɛ 'mɔgɛ ɔ'dmuvʲitɕ] |
| I'd be happy to. | **Z radością.**<br>[z ra'dɔɕtɕiɔ̃] |
| With pleasure. | **Z przyjemnością.**<br>[s pʃijɛ'mnɔɕtɕiɔ̃] |

# Refusal. Expressing doubt

| | |
|---|---|
| No. | **Nie.**<br>[ɲɛ] |
| Certainly not. | **Z pewnością nie.**<br>[s pɛ'vnɔɕtɕiɔ̃ 'ɲɛ] |
| I don't agree. | **Nie zgadzam się.**<br>[ɲɛ 'zgadzam ɕiɛ] |
| I don't think so. | **Nie wydaje mi się.**<br>[ɲɛ vɨ'dajɛ mʲi ɕiɛ] |
| It's not true. | **To nie prawda.**<br>[tɔ ɲɛ 'pravda] |
| You are wrong. | **Nie ma pan /pani/ racji.**<br>[ɲɛ ma pan /'paɲi/ 'ratsji] |
| I think you are wrong. | **Myślę że nie ma pan /pani/ racji.**<br>['mɨɕlɛ 'ʒɛ ɲɛ ma pan /'paɲi/ 'ratsji] |
| I'm not sure. | **Nie jestem pewien /pewna/.**<br>[ɲɛ 'jɛstɛm 'pɛvʲɛn /'pɛvna/] |
| It's impossible. | **To niemożliwe.**<br>[tɔ ɲɛmɔ'ʒʎivɛ] |
| Nothing of the kind (sort)! | **Nic podobnego!**<br>['ɲits pɔdɔ'bnɛgɔ!] |
| The exact opposite. | **Dokładnie odwrotnie.**<br>[dɔ'kwadɲɛ ɔ'dvrɔtɲɛ] |
| I'm against it. | **Nie zgadzam się.**<br>[ɲɛ 'zgadzam ɕiɛ] |
| I don't care. | **Wszystko mi jedno.**<br>['fʃistkɔ mʲi 'jɛdnɔ] |
| I have no idea. | **Nie mam pojęcia.**<br>[ɲɛ 'mam pɔ'jɛntɕa] |
| I doubt that. | **Wątpię w to.**<br>['vɔntpʲiɛ f 'tɔ] |
| Sorry, I can't. | **Przepraszam, nie mogę.**<br>[pʃɛ'praʃam, ɲɛ 'mɔgɛ] |
| Sorry, I don't want to. | **Przepraszam, nie chcę.**<br>[pʃɛ'praʃam, ɲɛ 'xtsɛ] |
| Thank you, but I don't need this. | **Dziękuję, ale nie potrzebuję tego.**<br>[dʑiɛn'kujɛ, 'alɛ ɲɛ pɔtʃɛ'bujɛ 'tɛgɔ] |
| It's late. | **Robi się późno.**<br>['rɔbʲi ɕiɛ 'puʐnɔ] |

I have to get up early.

**Muszę wstać wcześnie.**
['muʃɛ 'fstatɕ 'ftʃɛɕɲɛ]

I don't feel well.

**Źle się czuję.**
[ʑlɛ ɕɛ 'tʃujɛ]

# Expressing gratitude

Thank you.

**Dziękuję.**
[dʑiɛɲ'kujɛ]

Thank you very much.

**Dziękuję bardzo.**
[dʑiɛɲ'kujɛ 'bardzɔ]

I really appreciate it.

**Naprawdę to doceniam.**
[na'pravdɛ tɔ dɔ'tsɛɲam]

I'm really grateful to you.

**Jestem naprawdę wdzięczny /wdzięczna/.**
['jɛstɛm na'pravdɛ 'vdʑiɛntʃnɨ /'vdʑiɛntʃna/]

We are really grateful to you.

**Jesteśmy naprawdę wdzięczni.**
[jɛs'tɛɕmɨ na'pravdɛ 'vdʑiɛntʃɲi]

Thank you for your time.

**Dziękuję za poświęcony czas.**
[dʑiɛɲ'kujɛ za pɔɕvʲiɛn'tsɔnɨ 'tʃas]

Thanks for everything.

**Dziękuję za wszystko.**
[dʑiɛɲ'kujɛ za 'fʃistkɔ]

Thank you for ...

**Dziękuję za ...**
[dʑiɛɲ'kujɛ za ...]

your help

**pańską pomoc**
['paɲskɔ̃ 'pɔmɔts]

a nice time

**miłe chwile**
['mʲiwɛ 'xvʲilɛ]

a wonderful meal

**doskonałą potrawę**
[dɔskɔ'nawɔ̃ pɔ'travɛ]

a pleasant evening

**miły wieczór**
['mʲiwɨ 'vʲetʃur]

a wonderful day

**wspaniały dzień**
[fspa'ɲawɨ 'dʑɛɲ]

an amazing journey

**miła podróż**
['mʲiwa 'pɔdruʒ]

Don't mention it.

**Nie ma za co.**
[ɲɛ ma za 'tsɔ]

You are welcome.

**Proszę.**
['prɔʃɛ]

Any time.

**Zawsze do usług.**
['zafʃɛ dɔ 'uswuk]

My pleasure.

**Cała przyjemność po mojej stronie.**
[tsawa pʃi'jɛmnɔɕtɕ pɔ 'mɔjɛj 'strɔɲɛ]

Forget it. It's alright.

**Nie ma o czy mówić.**
[ɲɛ ma ɔ tʃi 'muvʲitɕ]

Don't worry about it.

**Nic nie szkodzi.**
['ɲits ɲɛ 'ʃkɔdʑi]

# Congratulations. Best wishes

Congratulations!

Happy birthday!

Merry Christmas!

Happy New Year!

**Gratulacje!**
[gratu'latsjɛ!]

**Wszystkiego najlepszego
z okazji urodzin!**
[fʃɪ'stkⁱɛgɔ najlɛ'pʃɛgɔ
z ɔ'kazjɪ u'rɔdʑin!]

**Wesołych Świąt!**
[vɛ'sɔwix 'ɕvⁱiɔnt!]

**Szczęśliwego Nowego Roku!**
[ʃtʃɛ̃ɕʎi'vɛgɔ nɔ'vɛgɔ 'rɔku!]

Happy Easter!

Happy Hanukkah!

**Wesołych Świąt Wielkanocnych!**
[vɛ'sɔwix 'ɕvⁱiɔnt vⁱɛlka'nɔtsnix!]

**Szczęśliwego Chanuka!**
[ʃtʃɛ̃ɕʎi'vɛgɔ 'xanuka!]

I'd like to propose a toast.

Cheers!

Let's drink to ...!

To our success!

To your success!

**Chciałbym wznieść toast.**
['xtɕawbɪm 'vzɲɛɕtɕ 'tɔast]

**Na zdrowie!**
[na 'zdrɔvⁱɛ!]

**Wypijmy za ...!**
[vɪ'pⁱijmɪ za ...!]

**Za naszą pomyślność!**
[za 'naʃɔ̃ pɔ'miɕlnɔɕtɕ!]

**Za Państwa pomyślność!**
[za 'paɲstfa pɔ'miɕlnɔɕtɕ!]

Good luck!

Have a nice day!

Have a good holiday!

Have a safe journey!

I hope you get better soon!

**Powodzenia!**
[pɔvɔ'dzɛɲa!]

**Miłego dnia!**
['mⁱiwɛgɔ 'dɲa!]

**Miłych wakacji!**
['mⁱiwix va'katsji!]

**Bezpiecznej podróży!**
[bɛ'spⁱɛtʃnɛj pɔ'druʒi!]

**Szybkiego powrotu do zdrowia!**
[ʃɪ'pkⁱɛgɔ pɔ'vrɔtu dɔ 'zdrɔvⁱa!]

# Socializing

Why are you sad?
**Dlaczego jest pani smutna?**
[dla'tʃɛgɔ 'jɛst 'paɲi 'smutna?]

Smile! Cheer up!
**Proszę się uśmiechnąć, głowa do góry!**
['prɔʃɛ ɕiɛ u'ɕmiɛxnɔntɕ, 'gwɔva dɔ 'guri!]

Are you free tonight?
**Czy ma pani czas dzisiaj wieczorem?**
[tʃi ma 'paɲi 'tʃaz 'dʑiɕaj viɛ'tʃɔrɛm?]

May I offer you a drink?
**Czy mogę zaproponować pani drinka?**
[tʃi 'mɔgɛ zaprɔpɔ'nɔvatɕ 'paɲi 'drinka?]

Would you like to dance?
**Czy mogę prosić do tańca?**
[tʃi 'mɔgɛ 'prɔɕitɕ dɔ 'taɲtsa?]

Let's go to the movies.
**Może pójdziemy do kina?**
['mɔʒɛ pu'jdʑɛmi dɔ 'kina?]

May I invite you to ...?
**Czy mogę zaprosić pani ...?**
[tʃi 'mɔgɛ za'prɔɕitɕ 'paɲi ...?]

a restaurant
**do restauracji**
[dɔ rɛsta'wratsji]

the movies
**do kina**
[dɔ 'kina]

the theater
**do teatru**
[dɔ tɛ'atru]

go for a walk
**na spacer**
[na 'spatsɛr]

At what time?
**O której godzinie?**
[ɔ 'kturɛj gɔ'dʑiɲɛ?]

tonight
**dziś wieczorem**
['dʑiɕ viɛ'tʃɔrɛm]

at six
**o szóstej**
[ɔ 'ʃustɛj]

at seven
**o siódmej**
[ɔ 'ɕudmɛj]

at eight
**o ósmej**
[ɔ 'usmɛj]

at nine
**o dziewiątej**
[ɔ dʑɛ'viɔntɛj]

Do you like it here?
**Czy podoba się panu /pani/ tutaj?**
[tʃi pɔ'dɔba ɕiɛ 'panu /'paɲi/ 'tutaj?]

Are you here with someone?
**Czy jest tu pani z kimś?**
[tʃi 'jɛst tu 'paɲi s 'kimɕ?]

| | |
|---|---|
| I'm with my friend. | **Jestem z przyjacielem /przyjaciółką/.** ['jɛstɛm s pʃija'tɕɛlɛm /pʃija'tɕuwkɔ̃/] |
| I'm with my friends. | **Jestem z przyjaciółmi.** ['jɛstɛm s pʃija'tɕuwmʲi] |
| No, I'm alone. | **Nie, jestem sam /sama/.** [ɲɛ, 'jɛstɛm 'sam /'sama/] |

| | |
|---|---|
| Do you have a boyfriend? | **Czy masz chłopaka?** [tʃi 'maʃ xwɔ'paka?] |
| I have a boyfriend. | **Mam chłopaka.** [mam xwɔ'paka] |
| Do you have a girlfriend? | **Czy masz dziewczynę?** [tʃi 'maʃ dʑɛ'ftʃinɛ?] |
| I have a girlfriend. | **Mam dziewczynę.** [mam dʑɛ'ftʃinɛ] |

| | |
|---|---|
| Can I see you again? | **Czy mogę cię jeszcze zobaczyć?** [tʃi 'mɔgɛ tɕiɛ 'jɛʃtʃɛ zɔ'batʃitɕ?] |
| Can I call you? | **Czy mogę do ciebie zadzwonić?** [tʃi 'mɔgɛ dɔ 'tɕɛbʲɛ za'dzvɔɲitɕ?] |
| Call me. (Give me a call.) | **Zadzwoń do mnie.** ['zadzvɔɲ dɔ 'mɲɛ] |
| What's your number? | **Jaki masz numer?** ['jakʲi 'maʃ 'numɛr?] |
| I miss you. | **Tęsknię za Tobą.** ['tɛ̃skɲiɛ za 'tɔbɔ̃] |

| | |
|---|---|
| You have a beautiful name. | **Ma pan /pani/ piękne imię.** [ma pan /'paɲi/ 'pʲiɛŋknɛ 'imʲiɛ] |
| I love you. | **Kocham cię.** ['kɔxam tɕiɛ] |
| Will you marry me? | **Czy wyjdziesz za mnie?** [tʃi 'vijdʑɛʃ za 'mɲɛ?] |
| You're kidding! | **Żartuje pan /pani/!** [ʒar'tujɛ pan /'paɲi/!] |
| I'm just kidding. | **Żartuję.** [ʒar'tujɛ] |

| | |
|---|---|
| Are you serious? | **Czy mówi pan /pani/ poważnie?** [tʃi 'muvʲi pan /'paɲi/ pɔ'vaʒɲɛ?] |
| I'm serious. | **Mówię poważnie.** ['muvʲiɛ pɔ'vaʒɲɛ] |
| Really?! | **Naprawdę?!** [na'pravdɛ?!] |
| It's unbelievable! | **To niemożliwe!** [tɔ ɲɛmɔ'ʑʎivɛ!] |
| I don't believe you. | **Nie wierzę.** [ɲɛ 'vʲɛʒɛ] |
| I can't. | **Nie mogę.** [ɲɛ 'mɔgɛ] |
| I don't know. | **Nie wiem.** [ɲɛ 'vʲɛm] |

I don't understand you.

**Nie rozumiem.**
[ɲɛ rɔ'zumʲɛm]

Please go away.

**Proszę odejść.**
['prɔʃɛ 'ɔdɛjɕtɕ]

Leave me alone!

**Proszę zostawić mnie w spokoju!**
['prɔʃɛ zɔ'stavʲitɕ 'mɲɛ f spɔ'kɔju!]

I can't stand him.

**Nie znoszę go.**
[ɲɛ 'znɔʃɛ 'gɔ]

You are disgusting!

**Jest pan obrzydliwy!**
['jɛst pan ɔbʒɨ'dʎivi!]

I'll call the police!

**Zadzwonię po policję!**
[za'dzvɔɲiɛ pɔ pɔ'ʎitsjɛ!]

# Sharing impressions. Emotions

I like it.
**Podoba mi się to.**
[pɔ'dɔba mʲi ɕiɛ 'tɔ]

Very nice.
**Bardzo ładne.**
['bardzɔ 'wadnɛ]

That's great!
**Wspaniale!**
[fspa'ɲalɛ!]

It's not bad.
**Nieźle.**
['ɲɛʑlɛ]

I don't like it.
**Nie podoba mi się to.**
[ɲɛ pɔ'dɔba mʲi ɕiɛ 'tɔ]

It's not good.
**Nieładnie.**
[ɲɛ'wadɲɛ]

It's bad.
**To jest złe.**
[tɔ 'jɛsd 'zwɛ]

It's very bad.
**To bardzo złe.**
[tɔ 'bardzɔ 'zwɛ]

It's disgusting.
**To obrzydliwe.**
[tɔ ɔbʒi'dʎivɛ]

I'm happy.
**Jestem szczęśliwy /szczęśliwa/.**
['jɛstɛm ʃʧɛ'ɕʎivi /ʃʧɛ'ɕʎiva/]

I'm content.
**Jestem zadowolony /zadowolona/.**
['jɛstɛm zadɔvɔ'lɔni /zadɔvɔ'lɔna/]

I'm in love.
**Jestem zakochany /zakochana/.**
['jɛstɛm zakɔ'xani /zakɔ'xana/]

I'm calm.
**Jestem spokojny /spokojna/.**
['jɛstɛm spɔ'kɔjni /spɔ'kɔjna/]

I'm bored.
**Jestem znudzony /znudzona/.**
['jɛstɛm znu'dzɔni /znu'dzɔna/]

I'm tired.
**Jestem zmęczony /zmęczona/.**
['jɛstɛm zmɛ'nʧɔni /zmɛ'nʧɔna/]

I'm sad.
**Jestem smutny /smutna/.**
['jɛstɛm 'smutni /'smutna/]

I'm frightened.
**Jestem przestraszony /przestraszona/.**
['jɛstɛm pʃɛstra'ʃɔni /pʃɛstra'ʃɔna/]

I'm angry.
**Jestem zły /zła/.**
['jɛstɛm 'zwi /'zwa/]

I'm worried.
**Martwię się.**
['martfiɛ ɕiɛ]

I'm nervous.

**Jestem zdenerwowany /zdenerwowana/.**
['jɛstɛm zdɛnɛrvɔ'vani /zdɛnɛrvɔ'vana/]

I'm jealous. (envious)

**Jestem zazdrosny /zazdrosna/.**
['jɛstɛm za'zdrɔsni /za'zdrɔsna/]

I'm surprised.

**Jestem zaskoczony /zaskoczona/.**
['jɛstɛm zaskɔ'tʃɔni /zaskɔ'tʃɔna/]

I'm perplexed.

**Jestem zakłopotany /zakłopotana/.**
['jɛstɛm zakwɔpɔ'tani /zakwɔpɔ'tana/]

# Problems. Accidents

I've got a problem.

**Mam problem.**
[mam 'prɔblɛm]

We've got a problem.

**Mamy problem.**
['mami 'prɔblɛm]

I'm lost.

**Zgubiłem /Zgubiłam/ się.**
[zgu'bʲiwɛm /zgu'bʲiwam/ ɕiɛ]

I missed the last bus (train).

**Uciekł mi ostatni autobus (pociąg).**
['utɕɛk mʲi ɔ'statɲi aw'tɔbus ('pɔtɕiɔŋk)]

I don't have any money left.

**Nie mam ani grosza.**
[ɲɛ 'mam 'aɲi 'grɔʃa]

---

I've lost my ...

**Zgubiłem /Zgubiłam/ ...**
[zgu'bʲiwɛm /zgu'bʲiwam/ ...]

Someone stole my ...

**Ktoś ukradł ...**
['ktɔɕ 'ukrat ...]

passport

**mój paszport**
[muj 'paʃpɔrt]

wallet

**mój portfel**
[muj 'pɔrtfɛl]

papers

**moje dokumenty**
['mɔjɛ dɔku'mɛnti]

ticket

**mój bilet**
[muj 'bʲilɛt]

---

money

**moje pieniądze**
['mɔjɛ pʲɛ'ɲiɔndzɛ]

handbag

**moje torebkę**
['mɔjɛ tɔ'rɛpkɛ]

camera

**mój aparat fotograficzny**
[muj a'parat fɔtɔgra'fitʃni]

laptop

**mój laptop**
[muj 'laptɔp]

tablet computer

**mój tablet**
[muj 'tablɛt]

mobile phone

**mój telefon**
[muj tɛ'lefɔn]

---

Help me!

**Pomocy!**
[pɔ'mɔtsi!]

What's happened?

**Co się stało?**
['tsɔ ɕiɛ 'stawɔ?]

fire

**pożar**
['pɔʒar]

| | |
|---|---|
| shooting | **strzał** ['stʃaw] |
| murder | **morderca** [mɔ'rdɛrtsa] |
| explosion | **wybuch** ['vɨbux] |
| fight | **bójka** ['bujka] |

| | |
|---|---|
| Call the police! | **Proszę zadzwonić na policję!** ['prɔʃɛ za'dzvɔɲitɕ na pɔ'ʎitsjɛ!] |
| Please hurry up! | **Proszę się pospieszyć!** ['prɔʃɛ ɕɛ pɔ'spʲɛʃitɕ!] |
| I'm looking for the police station. | **Szukam komendy policji.** ['ʃukam kɔ'mɛndɨ pɔ'ʎitsji] |
| I need to make a call. | **Muszę zadzwonić.** ['muʃɛ za'dzvɔɲitɕ] |
| May I use your phone? | **Czy mogę skorzystać z telefonu?** [tʃɨ 'mɔgɛ skɔ'ʒistatɕ s tɛle'fɔnu?] |

| | |
|---|---|
| I've been … | **Zostałem /Zostałam/ …** [zɔ'stawɛm /zɔ'stawam/ …] |
| mugged | **obrabowany /obrabowana/** [ɔbrabɔ'vanɨ /ɔbrabɔ'vana/] |
| robbed | **okradziony /okradziona/** [ɔkra'dʑɔnɨ /ɔkra'dʑɔna/] |
| raped | **zgwałcona** [zgva'wtsɔna] |
| attacked (beaten up) | **pobity /pobita/** [pɔ'bʲitɨ /pɔ'bʲita/] |

| | |
|---|---|
| Are you all right? | **Czy wszystko w porządku?** [tʃɨ 'fʃistkɔ f pɔ'ʒɔntku?] |
| Did you see who it was? | **Czy widział pan /widziała pani/ kto to był?** [tʃɨ 'vʲidzaw pan /vʲi'dʑawa 'paɲi/ 'ktɔ tɔ 'bɨw?] |
| Would you be able to recognize the person? | **Czy może pan /pani/ rozpoznać sprawcę?** [tʃɨ 'mɔʒɛ pan /'paɲi/ rɔ'spɔznatɕ 'spraftsɛ?] |
| Are you sure? | **Jest pan pewny /pani pewna/?** ['jɛst pan 'pɛvnɨ /'paɲi 'pɛvna/?] |

| | |
|---|---|
| Please calm down. | **Proszę się uspokoić.** ['prɔʃɛ ɕɛ uspɔ'kɔitɕ] |
| Take it easy! | **Spokojnie!** [spɔ'kɔjɲɛ!] |
| Don't worry! | **Proszę się nie martwić!** ['prɔʃɛ ɕɛ ɲɛ 'martfitɕ!] |
| Everything will be fine. | **Wszystko będzie dobrze.** [fʃistkɔ 'bɛndʑɛ 'dɔbʒɛ] |

Everything's all right.

**Wszystko jest w porządku.**
[fʃistkɔ 'jɛsd f pɔ'ʒɔntku]

Come here, please.

**Proszę tu podejść.**
['prɔʃɛ tu 'pɔdɛjɕtɕ]

I have some questions for you.

**Mam kilka pytań.**
[mam 'kʲiʎka 'pitaŋ]

Wait a moment, please.

**Proszę chwilę zaczekać.**
['prɔʃɛ 'xvʲilɛ za'tʃɛkatɕ]

Do you have any I.D.?

**Czy ma pan /pani/ dowód tożsamości?**
[tʃi ma pan /'paɲi/ 'dɔvut tɔʃsa'mɔɕtɕi?]

Thanks. You can leave now.

**Dziękuję. Może pan /pani/ odejść.**
[dʑiɛŋ'kujɛ. 'mɔʒɛ pan /'paɲi/ 'ɔdɛjɕtɕ]

Hands behind your head!

**Ręce za głowę!**
['rɛntsɛ za 'gwɔvɛ!]

You're under arrest!

**Jest pan aresztowany
/pani aresztowana/!**
['jɛst pan arɛʃtɔ'vani
/'paɲi arɛʃtɔ'vana/!]

# Health problems

| | |
|---|---|
| Please help me. | **Proszę mi pomóc.**<br>['prɔʃɛ mʲi 'pɔmuts] |
| I don't feel well. | **Źle się czuję.**<br>[ʑlɛ ɕɛ 'ʧujɛ] |
| My husband doesn't feel well. | **Mój mąż nie czuje się dobrze.**<br>[muj 'mɔ̃ʒ ɲɛ 'ʧujɛ ɕɛ 'dɔbʒɛ] |
| My son … | **Mój syn …**<br>[muj 'sin …] |
| My father … | **Mój ojciec …**<br>[muj 'ɔjtɕɛts …] |
| My wife doesn't feel well. | **Moja żona nie czuje się dobrze.**<br>['mɔja 'ʒɔna ɲɛ 'ʧujɛ ɕɛ 'dɔbʒɛ] |
| My daughter … | **Moja córka …**<br>['mɔja 'tsurka …] |
| My mother … | **Moja matka …**<br>['mɔja 'matka …] |
| I've got a … | **Boli mnie …**<br>['bɔʎi 'mɲɛ …] |
| headache | **głowa**<br>['gwɔva] |
| sore throat | **gardło**<br>['gardwɔ] |
| stomach ache | **brzuch**<br>['bʒux] |
| toothache | **ząb**<br>['zɔmp] |
| I feel dizzy. | **Kręci mi się w głowie.**<br>['krɛntɕi mʲi ɕɛ v 'gwɔvʲɛ] |
| He has a fever. | **On ma gorączkę.**<br>[ɔn ma gɔ'rɔnʧkɛ] |
| She has a fever. | **Ona ma gorączkę.**<br>['ɔna ma gɔ'rɔnʧkɛ] |
| I can't breathe. | **Nie mogę oddychać.**<br>[ɲɛ 'mɔgɛ ɔ'ddixatɕ] |
| I'm short of breath. | **Mam krótki oddech.**<br>[mam 'krutkʲi 'ɔddɛx] |
| I am asthmatic. | **Jestem astmatykiem.**<br>['jɛstɛm astma'tikʲɛm] |
| I am diabetic. | **Jestem diabetykiem.**<br>['jɛstɛm diabɛ'tikʲɛm] |

| | |
|---|---|
| I can't sleep. | **Mam problemy ze snem.**<br>[mam prɔ'blɛmi zɛ 'snɛm] |
| food poisoning | **Zatrułem się jedzeniem**<br>[za'truwɛm ɕiɛ jɛ'dzɛɲɛm] |

| | |
|---|---|
| It hurts here. | **Boli mnie tu.**<br>['bɔʎi 'mɲɛ 'tu] |
| Help me! | **Pomocy!**<br>[pɔ'mɔtsi!] |
| I am here! | **Jestem tu!**<br>['jɛstɛm 'tu!] |
| We are here! | **Tu jesteśmy!**<br>[tu jɛ'stɛɕmi!] |
| Get me out of here! | **Wyjmijcie mnie stąd!**<br>[vi'jmijtɕɛ 'mɲɛ 'stɔnt!] |
| I need a doctor. | **Potrzebuję lekarza.**<br>[pɔtʃɛ'bujɛ lɛ'kaʒa] |
| I can't move. | **Nie mogę się ruszać.**<br>[ɲɛ 'mɔgɛ ɕiɛ 'ruʃatɕ] |
| I can't move my legs. | **Nie mogę się ruszać nogami.**<br>[ɲɛ 'mɔgɛ ɕiɛ 'ruʃatɕ nɔ'gami] |

| | |
|---|---|
| I have a wound. | **Jestem ranny /ranna/.**<br>['jɛstɛm 'ranni /'ranna/] |
| Is it serious? | **Czy to poważne?**<br>[tʃi tɔ pɔ'vaʒnɛ?] |
| My documents are in my pocket. | **Moje dokumenty są w kieszeni.**<br>['mɔjɛ dɔku'mɛnti 'sɔ̃ f kiɛ'ʃɛɲi] |
| Calm down! | **Proszę się uspokoić.**<br>['prɔʃɛ ɕiɛ uspɔ'kɔitɕ] |
| May I use your phone? | **Czy mogę skorzystać z telefonu?**<br>[tʃi 'mɔgɛ skɔ'ʒistatɕ s tɛlɛ'fɔnu?] |

| | |
|---|---|
| Call an ambulance! | **Proszę wezwać karetkę!**<br>['prɔʃɛ 'vɛzvatɕ ka'rɛtkɛ!] |
| It's urgent! | **To pilne!**<br>[tɔ 'piilnɛ!] |
| It's an emergency! | **To nagłe!**<br>[tɔ 'nagwɛ!] |
| Please hurry up! | **Proszę się pospieszyć!**<br>['prɔʃɛ ɕiɛ pɔ'spiɛʃitɕ!] |
| Would you please call a doctor? | **Czy może pan /pani/ zadzwonić po lekarza?**<br>[tʃi 'mɔʒɛ pan /'paɲi/ za'dzvɔɲitɕ pɔ lɛ'kaʒa?] |
| Where is the hospital? | **Gdzie jest szpital?**<br>[gdʑɛ 'jɛst ʃpi'tal?] |

| | |
|---|---|
| How are you feeling? | **Jak się pan /pani/ czuje?**<br>['jak ɕiɛ pan /'paɲi/ 'tʃujɛ?] |
| Are you all right? | **Czy wszystko w porządku?**<br>[tʃi 'fʃistkɔ f pɔ'ʒɔntku?] |

What's happened?

**Co się stało?**
['tsɔ ɕiɛ 'stawɔ?]

I feel better now.

**Czuję się już lepiej.**
['tʃujɛ ɕiɛ 'juʒ 'lɛpʲɛj]

It's OK.

**W porządku.**
[f pɔ'ʒɔntku]

It's all right.

**Wszystko w porządku.**
['fʃistkɔ f pɔ'ʒɔntku]

# At the pharmacy

| | |
|---|---|
| pharmacy (drugstore) | **apteka**<br>[a'ptɛka] |
| 24-hour pharmacy | **apteka całodobowa**<br>[a'ptɛka tsawɔdɔ'bɔva] |
| Where is the closest pharmacy? | **Gdzie jest najbliższa apteka?**<br>[gdʑɛ 'jɛst najb'ʎiʃʃa a'ptɛka?] |
| Is it open now? | **Czy jest teraz otwarta?**<br>[ʧi 'jɛst 'tɛraz ɔ'tfarta?] |
| At what time does it open? | **Od której jest czynne?**<br>[ɔt 'kturɛj 'jɛst 'ʧinnɛ?] |
| At what time does it close? | **Do której jest czynne?**<br>[dɔ 'kturɛj 'jɛst 'ʧinnɛ?] |
| Is it far? | **Czy to daleko?**<br>[ʧi tɔ da'lɛkɔ?] |
| Can I get there on foot? | **Czy mogę tam dojść pieszo?**<br>[ʧi 'mɔgɛ tam 'dɔjɕʨ 'pʲɛʃɔ?] |
| Can you show me on the map? | **Czy może mi pan /pani/<br>pokazać na mapie?**<br>[ʧi 'mɔʒɛ mʲi pan /'paɲi/ pɔ'kazaʨ na 'mapʲɛ?] |
| Please give me something for ... | **Proszę coś na ...**<br>['prɔʃɛ 'tsɔɕ na ...] |
| a headache | **ból głowy**<br>[bul 'gwɔvi] |
| a cough | **kaszel**<br>['kaʃɛl] |
| a cold | **przeziębienie**<br>[pʃɛʑiɛm'bʲɛɲɛ] |
| the flu | **grypę**<br>['gripɛ] |
| a fever | **gorączkę**<br>[gɔ'rɔnʧkɛ] |
| a stomach ache | **ból brzucha**<br>[bul 'bʒuxa] |
| nausea | **nudności**<br>[nu'dnɔɕʨi] |
| diarrhea | **rozwolnienie**<br>[rɔzvɔ'lɲɛɲɛ] |
| constipation | **zatwardzenie**<br>[zatfar'dzɛɲɛ] |

| | |
|---|---|
| pain in the back | **ból pleców**<br>[bul 'plɛtsuf] |
| chest pain | **ból w klatce piersiowej**<br>[bul f 'klattsɛ pʲɛ'rɕɔvɛj] |
| side stitch | **kolkę**<br>['kɔʎkɛ] |
| abdominal pain | **ból brzucha**<br>[bul 'bʒuxa] |
| pill | **tabletka**<br>[ta'blɛtka] |
| ointment, cream | **maść**<br>['maɕtɕ] |
| syrup | **syrop**<br>['sirɔp] |
| spray | **spray**<br>['spraj] |
| drops | **drażetki**<br>[dra'ʒɛtkʲi] |
| You need to go to the hospital. | **Musi pan /pani/ iść do szpitala.**<br>['muɕi pan /'paɲi/ 'iɕtɕ dɔ ʃpʲi'tala] |
| health insurance | **polisa na życie**<br>[pɔ'ʎisa na 'ʒitɕɛ] |
| prescription | **recepta**<br>[rɛ'tsɛpta] |
| insect repellant | **środek na owady**<br>['ɕrɔdɛk na ɔ'vadi] |
| Band Aid | **plaster**<br>['plastɛr] |

# The bare minimum

| | |
|---|---|
| Excuse me, ... | **Przepraszam, ...**<br>[pʃɛ'praʃam, ...] |
| Hello. | **Witam.**<br>['vʲitam] |
| Thank you. | **Dziękuję.**<br>[dʑiɛŋ'kujɛ] |
| Good bye. | **Do widzenia.**<br>[dɔ vʲi'dzɛɲa] |
| Yes. | **Tak.**<br>[tak] |
| No. | **Nie.**<br>[ɲɛ] |
| I don't know. | **Nie wiem.**<br>[ɲɛ 'vʲɛm] |
| Where? | Where to? | When? | **Gdzie? | Dokąd? | Kiedy?**<br>[gdʑɛ? | 'dɔkɔnt? | 'kʲɛdi?] |

| | |
|---|---|
| I need ... | **Potrzebuję ...**<br>[pɔtʃɛ'bujɛ ...] |
| I want ... | **Chcę ...**<br>['xtsɛ ...] |
| Do you have ...? | **Czy jest ...?**<br>[tʃɨ 'jɛst ...?] |
| Is there a ... here? | **Czy jest tutaj ...?**<br>[tʃɨ 'jɛst 'tutaj ...?] |
| May I ...? | **Czy mogę ...?**<br>[tʃɨ 'mɔgɛ ...?] |
| ..., please (polite request) | **..., poproszę**<br>[..., pɔ'prɔʃɛ] |

| | |
|---|---|
| I'm looking for ... | **Szukam ...**<br>['ʃukam ...] |
| restroom | **toalety**<br>[tɔa'lɛti] |
| ATM | **bankomatu**<br>[bankɔ'matu] |
| pharmacy (drugstore) | **apteki**<br>[a'ptɛkʲi] |
| hospital | **szpitala**<br>[ʃpʲi'tala] |
| police station | **komendy policji**<br>[kɔ'mɛndɨ pɔ'ʎitsji] |
| subway | **metra**<br>['mɛtra] |

| | |
|---|---|
| taxi | **taksówki**<br>[ta'ksufkʲi] |
| train station | **dworca kolejowego**<br>['dvɔrtsa kɔlɛjɔ'vɛgɔ] |

| | |
|---|---|
| My name is … | **Mam na imię …**<br>[mam na 'imʲiɛ …] |
| What's your name? | **Jak pan /pani/ ma na imię?**<br>['jak pan /'paɲi/ ma na 'imʲiɛ?] |
| Could you please help me? | **Czy może pan /pani/ mi pomóc?**<br>[tʃi 'mɔʒɛ pan /'paɲi/ mʲi 'pɔmuts?] |
| I've got a problem. | **Mam problem.**<br>[mam 'prɔblɛm] |
| I don't feel well. | **Źle się czuję.**<br>[zlɛ ɕiɛ 'tʃujɛ] |
| Call an ambulance! | **Proszę wezwać karetkę!**<br>['prɔʃɛ 'vɛzvatɕ ka'rɛtkɛ!] |
| May I make a call? | **Czy mogę zadzwonić?**<br>[tʃi 'mɔgɛ za'dzvɔɲitɕ?] |

| | |
|---|---|
| I'm sorry. | **Przepraszam.**<br>[pʃɛ'praʃam] |
| You're welcome. | **Proszę bardzo.**<br>['prɔʃɛ 'bardzɔ] |

| | |
|---|---|
| I, me | **ja**<br>['ja] |
| you (inform.) | **ty**<br>['ti] |
| he | **on**<br>[ɔn] |
| she | **ona**<br>['ɔna] |
| they (masc.) | **oni**<br>['ɔɲi] |
| they (fem.) | **one**<br>['ɔnɛ] |
| we | **my**<br>['mi] |
| you (pl) | **wy**<br>['vɨ] |
| you (sg, form.) | **pan /pani/**<br>[pan /'paɲi/] |

| | |
|---|---|
| ENTRANCE | **WEJŚCIE**<br>['vɛjɕtɕɛ] |
| EXIT | **WYJŚCIE**<br>['vɨjɕtɕɛ] |
| OUT OF ORDER | **NIECZYNNY**<br>[ɲɛ'tʃinni] |
| CLOSED | **ZAMKNIĘTE**<br>[za'mkɲiɛntɛ] |

OPEN

**OTWARTE**
[ɔ'tfartɛ]

FOR WOMEN

**PANIE**
['paɲɛ]

FOR MEN

**PANOWIE**
[pa'nɔvʲɛ]

# MINI DICTIONARY

This section contains 250
useful words required for
everyday communication.
You will find the names of
months and days of the week
here. The dictionary also
contains topics such as colors,
measurements, family, and
more

**T&P Books Publishing**

# DICTIONARY CONTENTS

T&P Books Publishing

| | | |
|---|---|---|
| time | **czas** (m) | [tʃas] |
| hour | **godzina** (ż) | [gɔ'dʒina] |
| half an hour | **pół godziny** | [puw gɔ'dʒini] |
| minute | **minuta** (ż) | [mi'nuta] |
| second | **sekunda** (ż) | [sɛ'kunda] |
| | | |
| today (adv) | **dzisiaj** | ['dʒiɕaj] |
| tomorrow (adv) | **jutro** | ['jutrɔ] |
| yesterday (adv) | **wczoraj** | ['ftʃɔraj] |
| | | |
| Monday | **poniedziałek** (m) | [pɔne'dʒiawɛk] |
| Tuesday | **wtorek** (m) | ['ftɔrɛk] |
| Wednesday | **środa** (ż) | ['ɕrɔda] |
| Thursday | **czwartek** (m) | ['tʃfartɛk] |
| Friday | **piątek** (m) | [põtɛk] |
| Saturday | **sobota** (ż) | [sɔ'bɔta] |
| Sunday | **niedziela** (ż) | [ne'dʒeʎa] |
| | | |
| day | **dzień** (m) | [dʒeɲ] |
| working day | **dzień** (m) **roboczy** | [dʒeɲ rɔ'bɔtʃi] |
| public holiday | **dzień** (m) **świąteczny** | [dʒeɲ ɕfõ'tɛtʃni] |
| weekend | **weekend** (m) | [u'ikɛnt] |
| | | |
| week | **tydzień** (m) | ['tidʒeɲ] |
| last week (adv) | **w zeszłym tygodniu** | [v 'zɛʃwim ti'gɔdny] |
| next week (adv) | **w następnym tygodniu** | [v nas'tɛpnim ti'gɔdny] |
| | | |
| in the morning | **rano** | ['ranɔ] |
| in the afternoon | **po południu** | [pɔ pɔ'wudny] |
| | | |
| in the evening | **wieczorem** | [vet'ʃɔrɛm] |
| tonight (this evening) | **dzisiaj wieczorem** | [dʒiɕaj vet'ʃɔrɛm] |
| | | |
| at night | **w nocy** | [v 'nɔtsi] |
| midnight | **północ** (ż) | ['puwnɔts] |
| | | |
| January | **styczeń** (m) | ['stitʃɛɲ] |
| February | **luty** (m) | ['lyti] |
| March | **marzec** (m) | ['maʒɛts] |
| April | **kwiecień** (m) | ['kfetʃeɲ] |
| May | **maj** (m) | [maj] |
| June | **czerwiec** (m) | ['tʃɛrvets] |
| | | |
| July | **lipiec** (m) | ['lipets] |
| August | **sierpień** (m) | ['ɕerpeɲ] |

| September | wrzesień (m) | ['vʒɛɕeɲ] |
| October | październik (m) | [paʑ'dʒernik] |
| November | listopad (m) | [lis'tɔpat] |
| December | grudzień (m) | ['grudʒeɲ] |

| in spring | wiosną | ['vɔsnɔ̃] |
| in summer | latem | ['ʎatɛm] |
| in fall | jesienią | [e'ɕenɔ̃] |
| in winter | zimą | ['ʒimɔ̃] |

| month | miesiąc (m) | ['meɕɔ̃ts] |
| season (summer, etc.) | sezon (m) | ['sɛzɔn] |
| year | rok (m) | [rɔk] |

## 2. Numbers. Numerals

| 0 zero | zero | ['zɛrɔ] |
| 1 one | jeden | ['edɛn] |
| 2 two | dwa | [dva] |
| 3 three | trzy | [tʃi] |
| 4 four | cztery | ['tʃtɛri] |

| 5 five | pięć | [pɛ̃tʃ] |
| 6 six | sześć | [ʃɛɕtʃ] |
| 7 seven | siedem | ['ɕedɛm] |
| 8 eight | osiem | ['ɔɕem] |
| 9 nine | dziewięć | ['dʒevɛ̃tʃ] |
| 10 ten | dziesięć | ['dʒeɕɛ̃tʃ] |

| 11 eleven | jedenaście | [edɛ'naɕtʃe] |
| 12 twelve | dwanaście | [dva'naɕtʃe] |
| 13 thirteen | trzynaście | [tʃi'naɕtʃe] |
| 14 fourteen | czternaście | [tʃtɛr'naɕtʃe] |
| 15 fifteen | piętnaście | [pɛ̃t'naɕtʃe] |

| 16 sixteen | szesnaście | [ʃɛs'naɕtʃe] |
| 17 seventeen | siedemnaście | [ɕedɛm'naɕtʃe] |
| 18 eighteen | osiemnaście | [ɔɕem'naɕtʃe] |
| 19 nineteen | dziewiętnaście | [dʒevɛt'naɕtʃe] |

| 20 twenty | dwadzieścia | [dva'dʒeɕtʃ'a] |
| 30 thirty | trzydzieści | [tʃi'dʒeɕtʃi] |
| 40 forty | czterdzieści | [tʃtɛr'dʒeɕtʃi] |
| 50 fifty | pięćdziesiąt | [pɛ̃'dʒeɕɔ̃t] |

| 60 sixty | sześćdziesiąt | [ʃɛɕ'dʒeɕɔ̃t] |
| 70 seventy | siedemdziesiąt | [ɕedɛm'dʒeɕɔ̃t] |
| 80 eighty | osiemdziesiąt | [ɔɕem'dʒeɕɔ̃t] |
| 90 ninety | dziewięćdziesiąt | [dʒevɛ̃'dʒeɕɔ̃t] |
| 100 one hundred | sto | [stɔ] |

| | | |
|---|---|---|
| 200 two hundred | dwieście | ['dvɛɕtʃe] |
| 300 three hundred | trzysta | ['tʃista] |
| 400 four hundred | czterysta | ['tʃtɛrista] |
| 500 five hundred | pięćset | ['pɛtʃsɛt] |

| | | |
|---|---|---|
| 600 six hundred | sześćset | ['ʃɛɕtʃsɛt] |
| 700 seven hundred | siedemset | ['ɕedɛmsɛt] |
| 800 eight hundred | osiemset | [ɔ'ɕemsɛt] |
| 900 nine hundred | dziewięćset | ['dʒevɛ̃tʃsɛt] |
| 1000 one thousand | tysiąc | ['tiɕɔ̃ts] |

| | | |
|---|---|---|
| 10000 ten thousand | dziesięć tysięcy | ['dʒeɕɛtʃ ti'ɕentsi] |
| one hundred thousand | sto tysięcy | [stɔ ti'ɕentsi] |

| | | |
|---|---|---|
| million | milion | ['miʎjɔn] |
| billion | miliard | ['miʎjart] |

## 3. Humans. Family

| | | |
|---|---|---|
| man (adult male) | mężczyzna (m) | [mɛ̃ʃt'ʃizna] |
| young man | młodzieniec (m) | [mwɔ'dʒenets] |
| woman | kobieta (ż) | [kɔ'beta] |
| girl (young woman) | dziewczyna (ż) | [dʒeft'ʃina] |
| old man | staruszek (m) | [sta'ruʃɛk] |
| old woman | staruszka (ż) | [sta'ruʃka] |

| | | |
|---|---|---|
| mother | matka (ż) | ['matka] |
| father | ojciec (m) | ['ɔjtʃets] |
| son | syn (m) | [sin] |
| daughter | córka (ż) | ['tsurka] |
| brother | brat (m) | [brat] |
| sister | siostra (ż) | ['ɕɔstra] |

| | | |
|---|---|---|
| parents | rodzice (l.mn.) | [rɔ'dʒitsɛ] |
| child | dziecko (n) | ['dʒetskɔ] |
| children | dzieci (l.mn.) | ['dʒetʃi] |
| stepmother | macocha (ż) | [ma'tsɔha] |
| stepfather | ojczym (m) | ['ɔjtʃim] |

| | | |
|---|---|---|
| grandmother | babcia (ż) | ['babtʃʲa] |
| grandfather | dziadek (m) | ['dʒʲadɛk] |
| grandson | wnuk (m) | [vnuk] |
| granddaughter | wnuczka (ż) | ['vnutʃka] |
| grandchildren | wnuki (l.mn.) | ['vnuki] |
| uncle | wujek (m) | ['vuek] |
| aunt | ciocia (ż) | ['tʃɔtʃʲa] |
| nephew | bratanek (m), siostrzeniec (m) | [bra'tanɛk], [sɔst'ʃenets] |
| niece | bratanica (ż), siostrzenica (ż) | [brata'nitsa], [sɔst'ʃenitsa] |

| wife | żona (ż) | ['ʒɔna] |
| husband | mąż (m) | [mɔ̃ʃ] |
| married (masc.) | żonaty | [ʒɔ'nati] |
| married (fem.) | zamężna | [za'mɛnʒna] |
| widow | wdowa (ż) | ['vdɔva] |
| widower | wdowiec (m) | ['vdɔvɛts] |

| name (first name) | imię (n) | ['imɛ̃] |
| surname (last name) | nazwisko (n) | [naz'viskɔ] |

| relative | krewny (m) | ['krɛvni] |
| friend (masc.) | przyjaciel (m) | [pʃi'jatʃɛʎ] |
| friendship | przyjaźń (ż) | ['pʃijazʲɲ] |

| partner | partner (m) | ['partnɛr] |
| superior (n) | kierownik (m) | [ke'rɔvnik] |
| colleague | koleżanka (ż) | [kɔle'ʒaŋka] |
| neighbors | sąsiedzi (l.mn.) | [sɔ̃'ɕedʒi] |

## 4. Human body

| body | ciało (n) | ['tɕawɔ] |
| heart | serce (n) | ['sɛrtsɛ] |
| blood | krew (ż) | [krɛf] |
| brain | mózg (m) | [musk] |

| bone | kość (ż) | [kɔɕtʃ] |
| spine (backbone) | kręgosłup (m) | [krɛ̃'gɔswup] |
| rib | żebro (n) | ['ʒɛbrɔ] |
| lungs | płuca (l.mn.) | ['pwutsa] |
| skin | skóra (ż) | ['skura] |

| head | głowa (ż) | ['gwɔva] |
| face | twarz (ż) | [tfaʃ] |
| nose | nos (m) | [nɔs] |
| forehead | czoło (n) | ['tʃɔwɔ] |
| cheek | policzek (m) | [pɔ'litʃɛk] |

| mouth | usta (l.mn.) | ['usta] |
| tongue | język (m) | ['enzik] |
| tooth | ząb (m) | [zɔ̃mp] |
| lips | wargi (l.mn.) | ['vargi] |
| chin | podbródek (m) | [pɔdb'rudek] |

| ear | ucho (n) | ['uxɔ] |
| neck | szyja (ż) | ['ʃija] |
| eye | oko (n) | ['ɔkɔ] |
| pupil | źrenica (ż) | [zʲre'nitsa] |
| eyebrow | brew (ż) | [brɛf] |
| eyelash | rzęsy (l.mn.) | ['ʒɛnsi] |

| hair | włosy (l.mn.) | ['vwɔsi] |
|---|---|---|
| hairstyle | fryzura (ż) | [fri'zura] |
| mustache | wąsy (l.mn.) | ['võsi] |
| beard | broda (ż) | ['brɔda] |
| to have (a beard, etc.) | nosić | ['nɔɕitɕ] |
| bald (adj) | łysy | ['wisi] |

| hand | dłoń (ż) | [dwɔɲ] |
|---|---|---|
| arm | ręka (ż) | ['rɛŋka] |
| finger | palec (m) | ['palets] |
| nail | paznokieć (m) | [paz'nɔketɕ] |
| palm | dłoń (ż) | [dwɔɲ] |

| shoulder | ramię (n) | ['ramɛ̃] |
|---|---|---|
| leg | noga (ż) | ['nɔga] |
| knee | kolano (n) | [kɔ'ʎanɔ] |
| heel | pięta (ż) | ['pɛnta] |
| back | plecy (l.mn.) | ['pletsi] |

## 5. Clothing. Personal accessories

| clothes | odzież (ż) | ['ɔdʒeʃ] |
|---|---|---|
| coat (overcoat) | palto (n) | ['paʎtɔ] |
| fur coat | futro (n) | ['futrɔ] |
| jacket (e.g., leather ~) | kurtka (ż) | ['kurtka] |
| raincoat (trenchcoat, etc.) | płaszcz (m) | [pwaʃtʃ] |

| shirt (button shirt) | koszula (ż) | [kɔ'ʃuʎa] |
|---|---|---|
| pants | spodnie (l.mn.) | ['spɔdne] |
| suit jacket | marynarka (ż) | [mari'narka] |
| suit | garnitur (m) | [gar'nitur] |

| dress (frock) | sukienka (ż) | [su'keŋka] |
|---|---|---|
| skirt | spódnica (ż) | [spud'nitsa] |
| T-shirt | koszulka (ż) | [kɔ'ʃuʎka] |
| bathrobe | szlafrok (m) | ['ʃʎafrɔk] |
| pajamas | pidżama (ż) | [pi'dʒama] |
| workwear | ubranie (n) robocze | [ub'rane rɔ'bɔtʃɛ] |

| underwear | bielizna (ż) | [be'lizna] |
|---|---|---|
| socks | skarpety (l.mn.) | [skar'pɛti] |
| bra | biustonosz (m) | [bys'tɔnɔʃ] |
| pantyhose | rajstopy (l.mn.) | [rajs'tɔpi] |
| stockings (thigh highs) | pończochy (l.mn.) | [pɔɲt'ʃɔhi] |
| bathing suit | kostium (m) kąpielowy | ['kɔstʰjum kɔ̃pelɔvi] |

| hat | czapka (ż) | ['tʃapka] |
|---|---|---|
| footwear | obuwie (n) | [ɔ'buve] |
| boots (cowboy ~) | kozaki (l.mn.) | [kɔ'zaki] |
| heel | obcas (m) | ['ɔbtsas] |

| | | |
|---|---|---|
| shoestring | sznurowadło (n) | [ʃnurɔ'vadwɔ] |
| shoe polish | pasta (ż) do butów | ['pasta dɔ 'butuf] |
| | | |
| gloves | rękawiczki (l.mn.) | [rɛ̃ka'vitʃki] |
| mittens | rękawiczki (l.mn.) | [rɛ̃ka'vitʃki] |
| scarf (muffler) | szalik (m) | ['ʃalik] |
| glasses (eyeglasses) | okulary (l.mn.) | [ɔku'ʎari] |
| umbrella | parasol (m) | [pa'rasɔʎ] |
| | | |
| tie (necktie) | krawat (m) | ['kravat] |
| handkerchief | chusteczka (ż) do nosa | [hus'tɛtʃka dɔ 'nɔsa] |
| comb | grzebień (m) | ['gʒɛbeɲ] |
| hairbrush | szczotka (ż) do włosów | ['ʃtʃotka dɔ 'vwɔsuv] |
| | | |
| buckle | sprzączka (ż) | ['spʃɔtʃka] |
| belt | pasek (m) | ['pasɛk] |
| purse | torebka (ż) | [tɔ'rɛpka] |

## 6. House. Apartment

| | | |
|---|---|---|
| apartment | mieszkanie (n) | [meʃ'kane] |
| room | pokój (m) | ['pɔkuj] |
| bedroom | sypialnia (ż) | [si'pʲaʎɲa] |
| dining room | jadalnia (ż) | [ja'daʎɲa] |
| | | |
| living room | salon (m) | ['salɜn] |
| study (home office) | gabinet (m) | [ga'binɛt] |
| entry room | przedpokój (m) | [pʃɛt'pɔkuj] |
| bathroom (room with a bath or shower) | łazienka (ż) | [wa'ʒeŋka] |
| half bath | toaleta (ż) | [tɔa'leta] |
| | | |
| vacuum cleaner | odkurzacz (m) | [ɔt'kuʒatʃ] |
| mop | szczotka (ż) podłogowa | ['ʃtʃotka pɔdwɔ'gova] |
| dust cloth | ścierka (ż) | ['ɕtʃerka] |
| short broom | miotła (ż) | ['mɜtwa] |
| dustpan | szufelka (ż) | [ʃu'fɛʎka] |
| | | |
| furniture | meble (l.mn.) | ['mɛble] |
| table | stół (m) | [stɔw] |
| chair | krzesło (n) | ['kʃɛswɔ] |
| armchair | fotel (m) | ['fɔtɛʎ] |
| | | |
| mirror | lustro (n) | ['lystrɔ] |
| carpet | dywan (m) | ['dɨvan] |
| fireplace | kominek (m) | [kɔ'minɛk] |
| drapes | zasłony (l.mn.) | [zas'wɔni] |
| table lamp | lampka (ż) na stół | ['ʎampka na stɔw] |
| chandelier | żyrandol (m) | [ʒi'randɔʎ] |
| kitchen | kuchnia (ż) | ['kuhɲa] |

| | | |
|---|---|---|
| gas stove (range) | **kuchenka** (ż) **gazowa** | [ku'hɛŋka ga'zɔva] |
| electric stove | **kuchenka** (ż) **elektryczna** | [ku'hɛŋka ɛlekt'ritʃna] |
| microwave oven | **mikrofalówka** (ż) | [mikrɔfa'lyfka] |
| | | |
| refrigerator | **lodówka** (ż) | [lɔ'dufka] |
| freezer | **zamrażarka** (ż) | [zamra'ʒarka] |
| dishwasher | **zmywarka** (ż) **do naczyń** | [zmi'varka dɔ 'natʃiɲ] |
| faucet | **kran** (m) | [kran] |
| | | |
| meat grinder | **maszynka** (ż) **do mięsa** | [ma'ʃiŋka dɔ 'mensa] |
| juicer | **sokowirówka** (ż) | [sɔkɔvi'rufka] |
| toaster | **toster** (m) | ['tɔstɛr] |
| mixer | **mikser** (m) | ['miksɛr] |
| | | |
| coffee machine | **ekspres** (m) **do kawy** | ['ɛksprɛs dɔ 'kavi] |
| kettle | **czajnik** (m) | ['tʃajnik] |
| teapot | **czajniczek** (m) | [tʃaj'nitʃɛk] |
| | | |
| TV set | **telewizor** (m) | [tɛle'vizɔr] |
| VCR (video recorder) | **magnetowid** (m) | [magnɛ'tɔvid] |
| iron (e.g., steam ~) | **żelazko** (n) | [ʒɛ'ʎaskɔ] |
| telephone | **telefon** (m) | [tɛ'lefɔn] |